Tango

Creation of a
Cultural
Icon

Jo Baim

INDIANA UNIVERSITY PRESS
Bloomington and Indianapolis

Tango

This book is a publication of

Indiana University Press
601 North Morton Street
Bloomington, IN 47404-3797 USA

http://iupress.indiana.edu

Telephone orders	800-842-6796
Fax orders	812-855-7931
Orders by e-mail	iuporder@indiana.edu

The paper used in this publication meets the minimum
requirements of American National Standard for
Information Sciences–Permanence of Paper for
Printed Library Materials, ANSI Z39.48-1984.

Manufactured in the United States of America

Library of Congress Cataloging-in-Publication Data

Baim, Jo.
Tango : creation of a cultural icon / Jo Baim.
   p. cm.
Includes bibliographical references and index.
   ISBN-13: 978-0-253-34885-2 (cloth)
   ISBN-13: 978-0-253-21905-3 (pbk.)
1. Tango (Dance)–Social aspects–History. I. Title.
   GV1796.T3B34 2007
   784.18'885–dc22
                          2006039032
1 2 3 4 5 12 11 10 09 08 07

To H.,
who teaches me
every day
the truest joy of
dancing
through
life.

CONTENTS

Acknowledgments

To adequately thank everyone who helped with this project would require a second volume (properly documented in the Bibliography, of course). Friends and family, you know who you are, and each one of you has helped far more than you know. To my fellow Benedictines, both Oblates and Sisters, thank you for teaching me the holy value of work as prayer—may this little book be worthy of the unwavering encouragement you have given me.

Thanks to the patient and helpful editors at Indiana University Press—you were a joy to work with. Deepest appreciation goes to my friend and colleague Karin Pendle, Ph.D., for her enthusiastic support of tango as a dissertation topic and her steady good humor and belief in me ever since. Also, my thanks go to all the kind and helpful people in Buenos Aires, especially Ariel and Sandra.

One of the best things about researching historic ballroom dance is that you actually get to do the dances. Thanks to Richard Powers, Dr. Patri Pugliese, Joan Walton, and all the dance friends for some exquisite turns around the floor and many irreplaceable memories, as well as shared sources and ideas.

Many thanks to Lesley and Fay for the boxes of pencils, years of friendship, and endless cups of coffee, and to Steve, Bendetta, and Karri for taking such good care of You Know Who. And to Henry—constant, loyal, faithful companion of his dancing mom, even if he literally does have two left feet.

Tango

Introduction

The history of the tango is a story of encounters
between those who should never have met.

—Marta E. Savigliano, *Tango and the Political Economy of Passion*

 If one asks very many people about the tango, certain common threads still appear quite often: the tango is a dance from Argentina; the music always has a habanera rhythm; all tangos are sad or dramatic or tragic in some way; and it originated among the criminal classes in Buenos Aires around the end of the nineteenth century. As is the case with most beloved cultural icons, the common image is based in truth, but, as is just as often the case, error creeps in when devotees know or remember only parts of the history. A number of limitations plague the preceding description. First, the texts of tango songs in Argentina had a cultural importance equal to that of the dance music. Second, not all tango texts are sad; many of the earliest ones are based on comic or satiric themes of urban life. Third, starting with the first young Argentine aristocrats to discover the tango, many have assumed that lower class means criminal class. This affixed an undeserved label to many of the originators of the

tango, particularly women. This particular myth is perhaps the hardest one to shake, since modern social dancers enjoy re-creating the roles of sultry seductress and steamy gangster, and those roles also provide theatre audiences with something in-stantly recognizable. Yet in an age when women wish to add their own stories to validated, recorded history, it is paradoxical that only their bad sides appear relevant to the history of the tango. Fi-nally, though the habanera rhythm identifies the tango for many, it did not originate with the tango. Also, its appearance as the consistent rhythmic foundation of the bass line lasted for a rela-tively brief time, although, ornamented and distributed through-out the texture, it remains an integral part of tango music.

A completely different aspect of tango history emerges in the various answers to the question, Whose tango is it? Many Argen-tines smile politely when one discusses the European tango of the years before World War I, and suppress a laugh at the modern ball-room styles of Arthur Murray and others. Yet to a dance historian, all these are at least *called* "tangos" and must be considered parts of the whole picture. The problem then becomes one of finding the links of style, steps, and music between one geographical area or period and another, and tracing the paths of transmission.

The tango's complex history begins with seemingly unsolvable mysteries. Perhaps the earliest reference to the tango as a dance is in some proclamations of the municipal court of Montevideo, Uruguay, which prohibited performing the *tangos de negros* in public.[1] The first extant description of the tango, from 1856, does not mention Argentina. This reference is in a Philadelphia dance manual and is attributed to a Parisian dance master.[2] The connection to Paris is an interesting coincidence in light of the later importance of the Parisian tango. Nevertheless, the 1856 description gives nodding acknowledgment to South America as the tango's place of origin, and it adds credibility to a theory that the earliest tango dancers knew the popular ballroom dances of the mid-nineteenth century and used some of their steps in the tango.[3] After this anomalous description, primary source material on the tango is difficult to find until around 1910, and almost impossible to find in Argentina itself. Many European dance manuals after 1900 refer to Argentine style, and Argentine sources provide some sociological and stylistic information. What the latter lack, much to the regret of choreographers and historians, are specific descriptions or breakdowns of the actual steps. Without such mechanics it is nearly impossible to reconstruct the earliest tango dances with any accuracy, even though dancers can perhaps approximate the style.

Apart from its use for dancing, tango music is very important to Argentine culture. Today, many people who do not dance at all are actively involved in performing, preserving, and appreciating tango music. In fact, tango music and texts had cultural importance some twenty years before the dance was exported to Paris as a symbol of Argentina. The tango as song has documented the spirit, culture, and struggles of a nation of immigrants and displaced natives, savoring and enjoying the loneliness and isolation of being foreign in their own country and feeling deeply the political and economic strife that has characterized Argentine life—particularly life in Buenos Aires—throughout the country's history. The tango even has its own vocabulary, Lunfardo, which was originally a patois of the minor criminal class and became the expressive language of choice for writers of symbolic and metaphoric tango lyrics. For example, the Lunfardo word for the aforementioned pleasure of wallowing in one's own gloom is *mufarse*.[4]

My visit to Buenos Aires in 1991 ended on the inaugural day of a University of Tango—a civic venture designed to encourage citizens and visitors alike to go deeper into the history, musical repertoire, and culture of the tango. There are also several smaller archives in Buenos Aires dedicated to tango music past and present and to the iconography treasured by the Argentine people. Each year, more people visit the grave of Carlos Gardel, Argentina's beloved tango singer of the 1930s, than the graves of

Figure A. A female *bandoneon* player in the San Telmo market of Buenos Aires, 1991. Author's photograph.

Juan and Eva Peron. The few remaining street musicians who entertain with tango played on the *bandoneon*[5] are valued mentors for a new generation just becoming aware of the tango's importance to Argentine identity and determined to preserve this heritage. Buenos Aires has its own civic tango orchestra, which gives well-attended noontime concerts in the downtown business district. Americans flock to Argentina, becoming increasingly careful to seek out real *milongas*[6] and neighborhood dance classes. One hopes that the proliferation of tourist shows geared toward the well-known stereotypes will not hide the wonderful neighborhood venues.

My hope in writing this book is to set out, insofar as possible, only that picture of the early world of the tango which can be drawn from original sources. It is a picture with holes, and with gaps. Some parts are slightly out of focus, and others are veiled. The biggest gaps are, of course, in the parts of the tango's history that take place in Argentina itself.

I want to be clear from the start that I make no argument with authors who seek to give a more complete picture of the early tango, especially authors born and raised in Buenos Aires and thus steeped in the culture. Nuance, oral history, and tradition can fill in admirably where printed source material is lacking. I have confined myself, as much as possible, to the relative terra firma of extant written source material in the hope of offering a fresh, strong, yet transparent foundation for the study of many sides of the tango, and a clear idea of what remains unknown, speculative, or unverified.

Thus my plan is to set out documentary evidence on the early history of the tango, to trace and compare the forms it has taken in various countries, and to look at its use by dancers, composers, and musicians in terms of meanings chosen and rejected, the roles its dancers have played, its place in society, and its use as a symbol for a people, a way of life, and a mood to be enjoyed by those who choose to embrace it. The scope of this work must then necessarily expand beyond Argentina to other countries and cultures that adopted and adapted the tango, paying attention to their versions of the dance as well. To do so is not to forget that this unique form of dance and music, which conjures up vivid images for almost everyone, is inherently Argentine and always retains some connection to its roots. For reasons of space, and because their stories are told in detail elsewhere, this work will not deal with Carlos Gardel, Valentino, Astor Piazzolla, or other famous persons who may immediately come to mind as representatives of more modern periods of the tango's history.

Popular culture reveals itself in a wide range of places, and researchers must be attuned to the possibility of finding valuable information when and where they least expect it. The main sources of comprehensive information about social dance and the etiquette of the ballroom are the many manuals written by dance teachers to attract and instruct pupils and to cement their reputations as masters of their art. In the nineteenth century, manuals typically covered such topics as the importance of dancing as a social grace; etiquette and rules of the ballroom, including directions for hosting a ball and information on proper fashions; basic dance technique and posture; explanations of individual dance steps and quadrilles, possibly one or more contradances or line dances; and occasionally some music. In the ragtime era (roughly between 1900 and World War I) the pattern is less set, as some manuals begin with a defense of the modern dances and others with some account of the author's own history. Ragtime manuals also include instructions for the individual steps and dances, and many include choreographies, but there are far fewer group or set dances. Rather than including the music itself, ragtime manuals might list titles of appropriate music. One new feature of ragtime manuals was the use of diagrams drawn as though one were looking down at footprints on the floor. These "follow the dancing feet" diagrams are still used today in many ballroom studios.

One scholar has made a great number of dance manuals available to fellow historians by means of photocopied reproductions, but few are readily available for the average person.[7] Occasionally one finds some examples housed in the sports or dance sections of urban libraries, and others might turn up in secondhand bookstores, but unless the search is extended by photocopy exchange with other owners, access to interlibrary loan, and a willingness to search diligently in the libraries and bookshops of more than one country, it is almost impossible to put together a comprehensive collection. Without such a collection for reference, amateurs involved in historic dance are apt to make sweeping generalizations based on local practices, thus obscuring larger issues and trends and reflecting only a limited sense of the repertoire.

Using dance manuals as documentation can be problematic, especially when dealing with the smaller manuals of the ragtime era, particularly those that focus on only one dance. Many of these do not list a publisher, date, or city, and they might have been self-published by their authors. Sometimes the only way to date

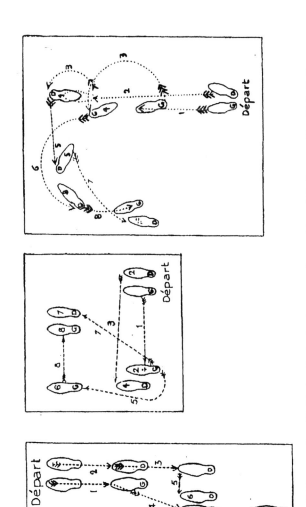

Figure B. Diagrams from D. Charles, *Toutes les danses modernes et leurs théories complètes* (Paris: S. Bornemann, 1920s): (a) the *Promenade Argentine*; (b) the *Pas battu de côté*; and (c) the *Spirale coupée* (explanations of the steps are found in appendix 1).

these volumes within a narrow period is to look at the women's fashions in the illustrations.

Gathering a collection of primary sources is only the first task. Beyond offering occasional diagrams of step patterns on the floor, dance manuals rarely use any kind of symbolic notation system, and steps are described in regular prose. This can be difficult to translate into actual movement, particularly for dance forms that were popular before it was possible to film dancers in action. Another difficulty occurs when a break in tradition has allowed steps to be forgotten and discarded rather than handed down with only slight modifications. Again, the more sources one can compare, the better the chance of correctly interpreting a step, since different descriptions of the same thing can lead to greater clarity.

Once enough sources from a given period have been examined, a dance historian has a picture of the dance repertoire that was presented to the public. Again, this is only a part of the whole, as this information represents only the dance masters' ideals for ballroom repertoire and behavior. To complete the study, many other kinds of sources should be consulted in order to acquire a sense of how the public received the dance masters' offerings—in other words, one must try to answer the question, But what did people actually do? Scholars must look at newspapers, magazines, artwork, other kinds of etiquette books, diaries, letters, dance cards, theatre programs, cultural histories, city directories that list dancing academies, fashion histories, and sheet music—and this list is by no means exhaustive.

One often-fascinating type of source material is the anti-dancing treatise. From the nineteenth century on, every time social dancing enjoyed a popular revival, there soon followed writings by any number of clergymen and social workers who blamed dancing for everything from divorce to prostitution. The frontispiece of one such treatise, written by a former dance master, reads: "MODERN DANCING and IMMODEST DRESS STIR SEX DE-

SIRE: leading to Lustful Flirting, Fornication, Adultery, Divorce, Disease, Destruction and Judgment." This might seem amusing to modern readers, particularly since the woman who is stirring sexual desire through her immodest dress is shown in the accompanying illustration to be clothed in a floor-length, long-sleeved, high-necked gown. The caption reads: "Only One of the Many Victims of the Church Parlor Dance."[8] One other comment from an anti-dance treatise is too delicious to exclude. In 1920 the evangelist Henry W. Von Bruch wrote: "You say dancing makes my daughter graceful. Thank God some mothers would rather their children waddle like a hippopotamus than to have their girls risk their honor upon a dance floor to learn gracefulness. . . . I would rather be a cripple on the road to heaven than an athlete on the road to hell."[9] Despite such hyperbole, these anti-dancing treatises often give detailed descriptions of ballroom behavior that contradict the propriety claimed by dance masters.

Newspapers and magazine articles give perhaps the best and, when taken as a group, the least-biased perspective on activity in the social dance world. A review of articles for or against a particular dance form reveals the trends of acceptance and rejection, whether general or varying from one place to another. Among the problems one encounters when doing research using newspapers published during the ragtime era is that many of the stories are simply silly, even though they provide accounts of how people thought about and reacted to the new dances. Also, unless one takes the time to search every major newspaper in several different countries, one is at the mercy of clippings files in the holdings of archives and libraries. In the case of the clippings files at the Lincoln Center Dance Library of the New York Public Library system, for example, clippings are grouped in files by subject, and then several clippings may be photocopied together on one page. Although the items on each page are clearly from the same time period, a significant number are without bylines, dates, cities, or newspaper names. This makes documentation difficult, but if a scholar's research has been wide enough in scope it is possible to know what the issues were and what kinds of events were taking place in a given period. Finding the same sorts of events, anecdotes, names, and places in magazine articles (which are much easier to date) also corroborates evidence drawn from newspaper clippings.

Sheet music can add a great deal of information over and above that of the music itself. Some pieces mention theatres or stage shows where well-known dancers performed to the music. Others include a brief, simple choreography that gives an idea of which steps from the dance manuals were accepted into the basic repertoires of the greatest number of people. The best-known tunes were mentioned in many clippings, articles, and dance descriptions; hence the publisher's date on the sheet music provides additional help in grouping together all the sources available. Fortunately, sheet music for dancing is in plentiful supply, as antique malls and flea markets usually have great quantities of unsorted music available. In addition, the Library of Congress, the Philadelphia Free Library, and the Newberry Library in Chicago, among others, have extensive cataloged collections of sheet music. Other sources of sheet music and orchestrations are the archives of radio stations that had live orchestras, such as the Seattle Public Library's collection from the old radio station KOMO.

Knowledge of fashions, especially women's ball gowns, is essential when a dance historian re-creates or reconstructs the steps of any era. It is possible to gauge the lengths of steps, the speed of turns, and many other aspects of historic dancing only if one knows, for example, the width, weight, and length of the ball gown's skirt and the height of the dancing shoe's heel, and all descriptions of posture and movement must be interpreted within the rules of clothing fashions and etiquette of each era. On rare occasions a dance inspired its own style of dress, such as the tango's narrow skirt with button closures at the back hem that could be opened out into a full pleat for daytime tango teas, or the bias-cut, draped skirt of the 1930s, or the Brazilian maxixe's requirement that women forgo wearing their corsets.

Other ephemera add to the matrix of social dance history. Dance motifs appear on matchbooks, floor-wax containers, tea canisters, stamps, flip books, and many other flea-market items. They help to show how widely a dance was known and how great a part of everyday life dancing was. It is the complete mix of everything a dance historian can find, from the most pedantic and scholarly treatise on dance to the silliest lyrics of a Tin Pan Alley tango parody, that creates an accurate picture of the history of social dance.

Researching the tango in Buenos Aires can provide scholars with some unique experiences. When I was there, many holdings in the main libraries were still cataloged on handwritten cards. Unless one is fluent in the Argentine dialect of Spanish, one is at the mercy of faded ink and idiosyncratic handwriting. Many resources in libraries, newspaper morgues, and other archives may be informally housed, and one must hope that the attendant on duty remembers seeing the required material. The tango, in addition, was not recorded in the kinds of books national and university libraries generally collect until the revival of interest in its history which began in the 1940s. The early tango historians—Ferrer, Gesualdo, Vega, Matamoro, Rossi, and others—were forced to rely on the memories of an older generation of witnesses and on ephemera from private collections. Much of this primary source material seems to have disappeared, or its location was either not recorded or has changed with the deaths of the collectors.

Reading accounts by early tango historians is fascinating but requires one to take a great deal on faith, as few documents or sources are cited. This is not surprising with a subject that for many years relied on oral tradition to convey its history; still, one would like to know more about the original documents, interviews, and memories upon which the writers relied. Since they were steeped in the tango from birth and generally were cultural historians whose perspectives were not fixed solely on the tango, they left a broad and fascinating tapestry drawn from local history, sociology, theology, and biography as well as the tango.

Resources for early tango music are more numerous and easier to find. A major collection of tango music in Buenos Aires is housed in the Sociedad de Argentina de autores y compositores. This archive, which is located in the same building as the office of the combined writers' and musicians' union, is a repository for works by Argentine artists. As was the case with nearly everyone from whom I sought help, the staff there was gracious and welcoming, and the acquisition of photocopies was a simple matter.

Each source found when researching the tango gives only a very small fragment of information. Like a mosaic, the whole picture is revealed only when all the pieces are in place. Unfortunately, in the mosaic of the tango, one must step back from those pieces that carry prejudice and misinterpretation to see clearly what the tantalizingly few gems of primary source material have to tell.

1 The Origins of the Tango

> The Tango is a dance of South American origin.
> —Charles Durang, *The Fashionable Dancer's Casket* (1856)

The People of the Early Tango

 The history of the tango is as elusive as the history of the Argentine people. Argentina is a country made up of persons claiming a mixture of, among others, Italian, Spanish, British, Basque, Irish, German, African, and native ancestry, with many shadings of caste and class. Unlike the United States, where a variety of ethnic identities can be preserved and hyphenated with "American," Argentina is a country whose people merged their various heritages with that of the native population to create a common Argentine identity. And unlike the United States, where native populations were driven out, early European arrivals to Argentina absorbed most native groups into the new society they built. Like most other societies, that of Argentina was stratified economically, and, especially in Buenos Aires, the least-urbanized natives were rapidly disenfranchised. Yet at the same time the various separate European threads quickly merged in the *porteño,* or citizen of the port city. The question is, Why did Buenos Aires gain both the prominence and the uniqueness that allowed the birth of such a distinctive cultural icon—distinctive certainly to Argentina, but even within Argentina, distinctive to Buenos Aires? Finding the answer requires at least an overview of how Argentina sorted itself out between the arrival of the first Spanish settlers and the turn of the twentieth century.

Early Spanish settlers in Argentina found resonance with the nomadic, cattle-herding native groups and intermixed freely with them. As more settlers arrived from Spain, however, the need for a greater Spanish administrative presence was felt. The imposition of the Spanish model of government introduced the idea of towns, most of which were built on the Spanish plan: a large church on one edge of the town square, surrounded by a few shops and businesses. Next would be a ring of large patio-style houses of wealthy families (some of which occupied a whole block). The outermost areas comprised progressively smaller houses of the lower classes.

Most of the wealthy families were of pure Spanish stock. Additionally, one of the wealthiest entities was the Roman Catholic Church. Not surprisingly, early Spanish settlers were given enormous land grants as well as positions of power and influence in both the church and the government. Wealthy monastic houses owned large properties and had control of education. Some larger towns had university-level schools run by monastic scholars. Thus, European ideas of culture and education were reserved for the wealthy, mostly Spanish class. By the nineteenth century, miscegenation laws preserved the wealth and family lineages of this privileged creole class.

Outside the towns, life centered around ranching. Under the *estancia* system, huge tracts of land were cheaply acquired but often difficult to control. The nineteenth century saw a gradual shift to sheep ranching in the north, as land was fenced in, with the *gauchos* (cowboys) and the more nomadic cattle herds moving further south. Whether it focused on sheep or cattle, the rural economy was based on meat, hides, and wool, with crop farming reserved for more coastal areas. These rural items formed the basis of Argentina's export market, although transporting goods to shipping ports took months by oxcart. Eventually, British-built railroads sped up the process considerably.

Buenos Aires gained early dominance as the major port city. As the point of entry for luxury European goods such as woolens, cottons, iron, and china, Buenos Aires quickly developed a taste for European styles and intellectual pursuits. The University of Buenos Aires—free of church control from its founding—opened in 1821. Literary, scientific, and charitable societies were numerous, and the latest dances and fashions from Paris were eagerly copied. While other inland cities such as Cordoba, Salta, and Tucumán were also cultural centers, they lacked the direct contact with European fashion and were quickly left behind.

Thus by the middle of the nineteenth century, several dichotomies were in place that made Buenos Aires unique even in its own country. The countryside was dominated by Spanish and native populations, while Buenos Aires was beginning to see the influx of immigrants from other countries. In the rural towns, wealthy families remained loyal to Spain and did not want political power centralized in Buenos Aires, while in the port city, liberal politics called for self-government. City life grew in variety and complexity with exciting new ideas and news arriving from Europe every day, while country life remained traditional and much more placid.

The rise to power of Juan Manuel de Rosas in the 1830s marked a brief return to a more conservative world. Rosas was pro-cattle and sympathetic toward the plight of the lower classes. He was against farming, industry, and liberal education. The biggest change for Buenos Aires was in the repression and censorship of scholarly debate, and many intellectuals fled. The church briefly regained some of the power in the cities that it had maintained in the countryside. Even so, Buenos Aires kept its European focus by continuing to import art and culture.

At mid-century, half of the population of Argentina lived in Buenos Aires or in the coastal region. Immigrants came as high-wage laborers, intending to earn a fortune and then leave. Many stayed, however, and brought new crops of wheat, corn, and flax to coastal farms. Trade continued, particularly with England. The British were given trade priority, and this status had important implications for British citizens working or living in Argentina: they could not be conscripted into the army, and they were allowed to practice their own form of religion.

By the third quarter of the nineteenth century, Buenos Aires began to receive large numbers of European immigrants. By 1900, two-thirds of Argentina's population was living on the coast or in the port city. The *mestizo* (mixed) class had largely been absorbed, the gauchos and nomadic groups had been driven south, the creole class was well established, and the shift to a Europeanized urban life was well under way. In the century's last two decades, massive development and public works projects were undertaken in Buenos Aires. By the 1880s, half of the streets were paved. Installation of electric lights and other new technologies kept pace with Europe and the United States. Arts and culture in the form of museums, opera, ballet, and theatre continued to grow. Intellectual freedom from church censorship was restored, and legislation passed in 1884 that prohibited priests from teaching.

Rampant inflation caused many of the public works to be halted. In May 1890 a group calling itself the Union Civica attacked the government, with three days of fighting in the streets of Buenos Aires. The lesson was learned, and the ruling oligarchy vowed to work for greater economic stability.

By 1900, three-quarters of the population of Buenos Aires was European-born. Each immigrant group had its own newspapers, social clubs, schools, and hospital. Even though these groups thought of themselves according to their country of birth, they were absorbed into *porteño* life and politics without any group making much trouble. Neighborhoods and districts developed according to immigrant origins and economic status, and frequently these barrios were largely self-contained with their own service industries. Other districts sprang up with other distinctions—significant to the tango is the downtown district of Corrientes, the site of many dance halls and nightclubs. Wealth counted more than birth in determining social hierarchy—the sons of wealthy sheep ranchers could move freely in the highest circles of Buenos Aires society. The sons of wealthy families were educated in Europe, and even daughters received a relatively broad education in arts and letters.

Thus Buenos Aires attracted many large groups of immigrants, who both melted into the local identity and consciously preserved their origins. The same could be said of New York, San Francisco, or any number of other port cities. What was it about Buenos Aires that prompted the invention of this unique dance form, the tango? What elements combined across the different cultures to make the tango the dance of all *porteños,* wherever their roots?

Argentina's multicultural history is relevant in many ways to the history of the tango, but the tango presents scholars with its own unique challenges. First, the tango can be traced to no single Argentine source. Many groups claim a connection to the etymology of the word *tango.* Some scholars of the history of the African diaspora link the word *tango* to an earlier word, *tambo,* the African term for the pens and markets where slaves were sold. Others retain the African link but attribute the word *tango* to a vocalization of the sounds of drums.

Those who place the tango's origins in the Cuban *candombe* or the Spanish (Andalusian) tango make similar exclusionary claims. More likely is a theory of combined influences that developed in a nearer parallel to that of the Argentine people, rather than an attribution to any single group. Buenos Aires, with the mismatched collection of people who populated its *conventillos* (tenements), was in some (occasionally unsavory) ways a truer melting pot than the United States ever was. The tango's original practitioners left no systematic documentation of its early history. In its early days it was referred to only by the literate classes, who were far distanced from life in the *conventillos,* except in the usual larks by privileged young men. Typically, such young men sought excitement, danger, and novelty in their outings and only encountered the seamier side of the tango. Thus only part of its history has been described in eyewitness accounts. One must search through documents written for other purposes to find anything approaching the whole story of the tango's origins and early history.

While the stage was being set for the collision of peoples who would produce the tango, Argentina's elite society was following the same path as the upper classes in Europe and North America. Musical life in Buenos Aires included performances of all the current operatic and concert works. A resident opera company was founded in 1848, and ballet was performed as early as the 1830s. Gottschalk and Paganini were among the artists who gave concerts in Buenos Aires; in addition, sacred music was very popular, particularly in the form of organ concerts.[1] Buenos Aires citizens of all classes participated in social dancing, learning the quadrilles, waltzes, polkas, mazurkas, and schottisches that were all the rage in nineteenth-century ballrooms. An African American dance teacher from the United States, Joseph William Davis, advertised himself in *La gaceta mercantil* on January 9, 1827, as a "professor of the north American dances, from the state of Rhode Island," and offered a pamphlet he had written explaining the quadrille. Davis ran a dance studio in Buenos Aires from 1827 to 1848 and returned to the United States, England, and France on at least one occasion to collect the latest repertoire of steps. Also, Theodore Rousseaux, who established the Academia de Baile del Comercio Republicano-Federal (Dance Academy of the Federal Republic) in 1839, introduced the polka in a production at the Teatro de la Victoria in 1845, and he continued for many years to introduce the latest social dances and ballets to Buenos Aires.[2] The popular ballroom dances at this time were not the sole property of the upper classes, and various newspaper notices survive that advertise dance classes all over the city. Thus, in addition to the *pericones* and other folk dances of the countryside, quadrille steps and formations, as well as polkas, mazurkas, and other dances, were available repertoire for the mix of people who created the tango.

Charles Durang's 1856 description of the tango as "a dance of South American origin," along with some obscure musical references, still belongs to the mists of history for the moment.[3] The search for the tango begins most successfully in the Buenos Aires of the 1880s. By this time a new group of people was forming in the port city, made up of persons who were displaced from their origins by choice or force and who did not find life in the city an improvement. Along with the *payadores,* whose tradition of exchanged insults in rhymed couplets contributed to the witty lyrics of later tangos, most of the gauchos of the pampas had by 1880 suffered one of three fates: conscription into the army, isolation on the ranch of some wealthy European *terrateniente* (landholder), or assimilation into *conventillos* in the poorer sections of Buenos Aires. Many of the *conventillos* had once been the typical large homes of the wealthy, but urban expansion left these residences to be divided by the poor into small apartments, and a whole community came to fill the waterfront where only a few privileged families once lived.

Within this community clashed different kinds of men. The gauchos, fresh from a macho culture on the pampas (where married men faced constant derision that they were something less than real men, who apparently only really needed, or loved, their horses), re-created themselves within the context of the new waterfront urban culture of Buenos Aires. These new fellows were called *compadritos* or *guapos*. Both words mean roughly the same thing: tough guys, probably armed with knives, not constant criminals but always on the edge of the law, with exaggerated dress and mannerisms. Typically, their costume included a homburg hat pulled low over the forehead, a fancy vest (sometimes with a watch chain), baggy trousers pegged in at the ankle, and buttoned half boots with a high, shaped heel. Some acted as pimps, although frequently the Lunfardo word *canflinflero* was used for men who controlled one or more prostitutes.

One of the most enduring myths of the tango, and one of the few that can definitely be proved false, is that it was actually the gauchos who danced the tango. Enrico Pichetti, an Italian dance master, spent several years in Argentina around 1900 and ran his own dance studio in Buenos Aires. He observed the development of the tango and, in his 1914 dance manual, stated emphatically that the gauchos did not dance the tango. By the time the tango was created, says Pichetti, the gauchos had been absorbed into the urban culture and were just one element in the group that had evolved into the *compadritos*. That Pichetti actually was in Argentina as he claimed is substantiated by mention of him in a 1902 cultural history of Argentina.[4] European immigrants, competing with these native citizens in the job market, adopted some of the ways of the *compadrito* and lamented their long-lost homes abroad. Natives of the country found little in the cities and sank to the lowest level of the urban society.

According to most demographic histories of Argentina, one of the biggest problems this new community faced was a shortage of women. Many sources give an average figure of five men for every woman in this class of Argentine society.[5] And, as usual at this time, the women had far fewer choices of ways to earn a living than the men. Prostitution, including white slavery, was the unfortunate fate of many.[6] Also, there was an equivalent to the

Figure 1.1. Unattributed artist's concept of a *compadrito,* from Ernesto
Sabato, *Tango: Canción de Buenos Aires* (Buenos Aires: Editiones Centro
Arte, 1964), n.p.

compadrito in the *mina,* an unmarried woman who was usually attached to just one man at a time and who filled in the time between attachments with prostitution. The *mina* is the usual female subject of tragic tango songs in the early days. As an archetype, she could be expected to betray her lover, possibly turning him in to the police, and her lack of fidelity was the source of the heartache expressed in many tango songs. Yet as with the *compadrito,* one should not assume a *mina* was always a hardened criminal. Often she was just a poor woman, sometimes a European woman who had been promised marriage and then had to survive after being abandoned, sold into prostitution, or forced into partnership with a petty thief once she arrived in Buenos Aires. Tradition has it that the *compadrito* was so charismatic that, until the *mina* turned him in to the police, her devotion to her man was absolute—in other words, theirs was a relationship based on extremes of emotion. Around 1900 the *compadritos* were heard to sing the following verse in tango rhythm:

> Pimp, leave that girl alone!
> And why should I leave her alone?
> If she arms me and clothes me
> And gives me food?
> She buys me stylish clothes
> And a soft hat like the *Oriental*
> And she also buys me boots
> With military heels.[7]

These archetypes of sordid gangsters and tawdry ladies of the evening quickly became stereotypes. With the sometimes narrow and judgmental vision of the privileged and literate class, those who described the early tango clubs saw only what their prejudice allowed them to see: criminals engaged in vulgar dancing. This image was then transported to the outside world, where it was received either with horror and dismay or with excitement and enthusiasm.

The tango-in-the-brothel scenario was further cemented in people's minds by Argentina's own beloved literary icon, Jorge Luis Borges. His vivid descriptions of life in Buenos Aires at the turn of the twentieth century have the ring of truth found in personal reminiscences. Yet in later life Borges recanted his description of the tango and allowed it a less objectionable history.

One of the most substantial primary source descriptions comes from a *libro rojo,* or banned book: the memoir of Adolfo Batiz, a Buenos Aires policeman, published in Buenos Aires early in the twentieth century.[8] Part of the book recounts his early manhood and his forays into the city's underworld. The following account sheds light on the murky personality of the *compadrito* and the world of the tango:

> There the *compadritos* gathered, a type that did no more damage than to exaggerate their style of dress, wearing half-boots with high heels, a narrow slouched hat, and scarves in flashy colors. The *compadrito* is part of the fringes of society. I want to state that he is not the *canflinflero* [pimp] of whom we spoke earlier. The *compadrito* worked, and frequented more places than the cosmopolitan brothels of the suburbs.
>
> One day in 1887 as I walked about, a suspect nicknamed Rata Carcelera [the name is a pun: *rata* = rat and *carcelera* = someone who posts bail for a prisoner], who used the same nickname when he gave the police business as a *quincenario* [the delinquents that the police arrested and detained for fifteen days as prevention were called *quincenarios*] was playing at billiards in the company of other individuals of his social class. I was stationed in the path in front of the Temple, facing the windows of the salon, and addressing myself plainly to Rata. I said to him: "You have many tricks, you are one of those tigers who plays well." In truth, he responded by smiling at me, which gave me the courage to continue the conversation on the theme of prostitutes. In roguish language we talked of the mulatta Loreto, a midwife of the kind we have already referred to, a fighter and an agitator; of Henrietta the Crafty One, another of the *chinas* [a

china is a half-breed or servant or gaucho's girl, etc.] famous for her bravery, who was given work on several occasions by the third Commissary, and who defended herself against the seducers by throwing glasses and bottles; and of the mulatta Refucilo, who was only a midwife and a *compadrita* and danced alone.

Rata and I laughed a little, and I interrogated him with several questions about how many houses of white slavery there were all together: I had been told that they did unnatural things in them. The devil of a *lunfardo* started laughing and answered me: there were 69 and others besides. He seemed to be saying nonsense. It followed that after an amicable and smiling goodbye, he rushed away until he reached the street door of one of these places, returning to me later to say some insulting words.

The *compadrito* is a type like Nemesio Menendez, without detectable antecedents, who has a fanciful and exaggerated style, with a high-heeled half-boot and a narrow slouch hat, generally with a peculiar or contrived appearance, with which he wants to make himself noticed. He wears a silk scarf around his neck; he might or might not have a shirt; he uses regional sayings and idioms; and lives in the suburbs, from where he also takes the name *orillero* [outskirter]. This is the *compadrito,* of obscure race that is neither black nor white.

The *compadrito* does not belong with the rich social bourgeoisie, nor with the *lunfardo* [thief] and pimp; he forms a special type that requires a special class.

He is, in general, inoffensive, and he works.[9]

Other unbiased writers also point out that the *compadrito* was not likely to be more than a petty criminal, since the whole reason for his exaggerated style of dress and mannerisms was to call attention to himself. A memorable *compadrito* would have had a very short career as a major criminal.[10] Part of the problem the *compadritos* had with the authorities was that many of them were enforcers for labor politics and could therefore motivate a voting bloc far greater than that of the establishment.

Batiz also describes a night on the town:

Upon arriving at the aforementioned corner I met up with several coachmen. We gathered on the sidewalk, and stopped a Neapolitan organist [organ-grinder] who was passing by at that moment. He proceeded to play the organ until noon, putting what he was paid into the neck of his shirt—a few cents from each person except me, as I carried in my pockets only cigarettes and matches.

I don't remember the names of those we encountered in that happy open-air party, except a few: Nemesio Menendez the *compadrito,* who at that time I thought to be like a *quincenario;* Adolfo Veroy, who had stirred up the consciousness for reforming conditions; the Porteño, a great person, short in stature, and a frequent participant in night wanderings; the Orillero, one of those who wore a knife at his belt; and the Garabito brothers. It happened that the musician entered into the fun and laughter even to the point of organizing a dance on the sidewalk, during which the *compadre* Nemesio, with Garabito the younger and Veroy, did many pirouettes and graceful postures. It lacked only the mulatta Loreto and the *china* Refucilo in order to call the dance a street festival, in which Nemesio was extravagant in eloquence and opportunity, with *criollo* postures and sayings. [It is possible that the coachmen danced an early form of tango and that Batiz, by reason of his youth, was ignorant of the name of the dance.]

The party ended at midnight, the gatherers at the Varieties began to leave. No one but the libertines remained, going into two or three of the avenue cafés where there were also gambling houses, and of the coachmen, only the Orillero, who invited me to accompany him. Moments later he was employed by someone. We set off heading north on Esmeralda, until we reached Juncal Street. On our route we saw that everything was closed and quiet. In the San Martin Plaza, solitary and majestic, covered with flowers and green leaves that perfumed the atmosphere, as spacious as Luxembourg or Paris, the aesthetic taste and the variety of plants intoxicated all with the melodies of the enchanted nights. We came to the Recoleta and the northern part of Buenos Aires. The neighborhood of the aristocratic palaces was silent, and we heard only the monotonous wheels of the carriages of those out all night with loose women and call girls, directing themselves toward Palermo, and in those times there were many such.[11]

While admittedly not describing a high-society tea, Batiz's story is that of a boys' night out—no harm done, no laws broken, no knife-wielding gaucho dying in a pool of blood calling out the name of his unfaithful mistress. The only libertines and customers for the prostitutes he describes are from the upper class.

As history, particularly cultural history, is examined from many different points of view and begins to include the stories of women and others traditionally without a voice, more and more writers recognize the limitations of Borges's paradigm. One such writer is Arturo Penon, a virtuoso player of the *bandoneon* and a thoughtful modern commentator on many aspects of the tango's history. He expands on the myths and stereotypes of the tango's earliest participants:

Here then is the courtyard, hung with cradles, cooled by a basin of water, and lit with kerosene lanterns. Far away, we can see the movement of hair buns, ribbons, and patent leather shoes. Coming a little closer, we can make out the regular customers mixing with the gatecrashers and hooligans, who've come to dance, wet their whistles, and play games of cards and seduction. Here we find alcohol, musicians, the neighbourhood singer, and floozies with their long nails and embroidered dresses. We could also point out the spats, the kerchiefs, the tailored pants, and the turned down hats, but it would be best to leave these in shadow so that the reader can imagine them in his own way. Everything is set for the mixing of *mate* and poker, of polkas and *pericones*,[12] and for declarations of love amidst the fray.

The tango, as I have already said, sprang out of the most humble quarters of the two cities of the River Plata,[13] far from the cities' centres and the neighbourhoods of the wealthy. While in the working class suburbs the search for an original style was pursued through disjointed and fragmented rhythms, a different music, part of a well-established tradition, lived on at the gatherings of so-called high society, in private salons or in chic nightclubs Viennese and French waltzes, the Cuban habanera and danzon, and dances of Spanish origin. In these circles the tango was considered indecent, and here lies the origin of the belief that the tango was born in the brothels. One of the most fervent defenders of this theory was our great writer Jorge Luis Borges. During the brief period of his interest in popular culture, Borges wrote an article on the history of the tango. This article began with a refutation of the "sentimental version" of that history, according to which the tango's origins lie in the working class neighbourhoods, and proposed instead—drawing on the writer's own personal recollections, and referring to the essentially "lascivious" nature of the dance and to the titles of some tangos of an obviously obscene nature—the theory of the tango's origins in the brothels.

It's paradoxical that the Borgesian brothel theory has become transformed with time into a veritable axiom. The majority of articles written today, by those who have arrived rather late to the study of the tango's history, and who only know it from the outside, start with this blueprint—which is in reality no more than the ruling class's image of the tango during the first decades of the century. It is the theory of a social group that can see the working class neighbourhoods only as an immense brothel. It is symptomatic, for example, that Blas Matamoro, one of the writers who adopts this theory uncritically, can write, on page 33 of his book *La ciudad del tango:* ". . . the middle class, poor like the workers but decent like the rich. . . ." It is this kind of thinking, essentialist and ingenious, and absolutely ignorant of the complexities of reality, that has allowed the theory of the tango's brothel origins to triumph. It's interesting to note how this theory presupposes direct links between poverty and indecency and between wealth and decency. It is the version of those who, at the turn of the century, shut the tango out of their lives.[14]

A description from the Buenos Aires newspaper *La nación,* October 20, 1880, tells of gatherings in the Plaza Constitución:

> By the flickering light of a kerosene lantern, people of both sexes play, drink, dance, and talk. Wine glasses run with liqueurs; they smoke local cigars (at eight for a peso); they eat chorizo sausages cooked on grills set up in doorways; they fry fish, and when the chords of the guitar, badly played by a drunken negro accompanied by an accordion, are no longer audible, a street organ, stopped in the pathway or intersection, makes its raucous notes heard. Police action is going to eliminate many of these hovels.[15]

In his memoir, Batiz touches on one of the unusual elements of the tango's early story—that of men dancing together. There exists a series of five photographs showing two men demonstrating a number of characteristic tango poses. Most aficionados of tango lore are familiar with these photographs, and there are multiple interpretations of their meaning. Those who believe the tango is solely a man's dance think that men practiced together and learned new steps from each other in order to perfect their skills before dancing with women, thereby protecting the male ego from the embarrassment of a misstep. Others believe that the learning process took place between men because of the fact that there were significantly more men than women in that part of Buenos Aires. Since each woman would have had at least several potentially skilled dance partners, newcomers needed to learn quickly, and no one would want to gain a reputation with the women as a novice dancer among so many experts. Learning between men was thus the safest way to acquire the needed repertoire of complex dance steps.

A less complex interpretation also relates to the disproportionate number of men: people simply like to dance, and just like the miners of the Old West, the leftover ladies at a ball, or count-less generations of teenagers, they will dance with whoever is available. This is consistent with Batiz's description: he and his friends would have welcomed the presence of women, but they went ahead with their street dance anyway. Since we do not know the source or purpose of the series of photographs, or ex-actly how widespread the practice was, it is impossible to deter-mine for sure how much the tradition of men dancing the tango together was a result of practicalities or a matter of macho pride. Another possible explanation is that the men in the photographs were merely demonstrating tango steps to someone with a cam-era. Again, there is no way to be certain. However, another series of photographs shows one of the same men in characteristic tango poses with a woman.[16] Whatever the reason, it did not go unnoticed by the Paris demimonde, as photographs also exist with well-known men spoofing the Argentine practice.

Lunfardo and the Language of the Tango

Lunfardo, the urban patois described in the introduction, influ-enced tango lyrics and helped to establish the stereotypical im-ages many people today hold of the tango's early participants. The themes of early tangos—family love, pure sex, social and po-litical criticism, and, attached to all of the above, betrayal—gave voice to the discontent and frustration of the lower class. Lunfardo as a new form of slang used by petty thieves first appeared in Buenos Aires in the late 1870s. Benigno Lugones, writing in *La nación* in March and April 1879, describes the slang used by a class of small-time criminals and uses the word *lunfardo* for both the thief and his language. The word may be a Spanish corruption of the Italian *lombardo,* a word used as a synonym for *thief,* and may reflect the growing presence of Italian immigrants in Buenos Aires at this time. Lugones gives fifty-four words in Lunfardo, claiming that by use of these words a thief would identify himself

Figure 1.2. Early tango dancers: three of a series of
five photographs of men dancing. From the Archivo
General de la Nación, Buenos Aires.

and the type of mark he was seeking. Donald Castro supplies a list
based on Lugones's work, from which the following are taken:

bacan = man/robber
bolines = rooms
escrucho = breaking and entering, done by an *escruchante*
lunfardo = criminal/thief
michos = poor people
mina = a woman, possibly part of a man/woman team of thieves
la musica = pocket watch
otario = mark, target for robbery

pillo = thief
punga = the art of pickpocketing, done by a *pungalista*
trabajar = to rob

In addition to introducing Lunfardo vocabulary to a literate audience, Lugones includes an example of early Lunfardo poetry:

> Esando en el bolin polizando
> Se presento el mayorengo:
> "A portarlo encama vengo
> su mina lo ha delatado."

> He was in the pad sleeping when
> The police inspector suddenly broke in.
> "I'm here to take you to the pen 'cause
> your lady has turned you in."[17]

In 1888, Luis M. Drago wrote a scientific study of Argentine criminals.[18] He also saw Lunfardo as an argot of the criminal class and pointed out that it uses a single verb to mean both "work" and "rob." Drago created a lexicon of Lunfardo, showing how the criminals viewed the world as divided into people, who were either easy or difficult to rob, and things, which either were or were not worth stealing. He concluded that Lunfardo was undergoing constant revision and was a creative hodgepodge of phrases, words, onomatopoeic combinations, and words taken from a wide variety of foreign languages.[19] Several others made criminological studies of Lunfardo thieves, but not until 1894 was an actual dictionary of the Lunfardo language compiled. That study, by criminologist Antonio Dellepiane, is of special interest to the study of the tango because it gave several examples of Lunfardo poetry, including the following:

> Cuando el bacan esta en cana
> La mina se pinta rizos;
> No hay mina que no se espiante
> Cuando el bacan anda micho.

When the man is in jail
His lady becomes a coquette;
There is no fluff that will follow her man
When he is down and out.[20]

This view of Lunfardo as the property of the criminal class continued until well after the turn of the century. Most of those who investigated Lunfardo were criminologists, and their studies of Lunfardo were means to the end of studying criminals. Adding in the expected biases of literate and professional classes toward the urban poor, their assumptions about the use of Lunfardo are perhaps not surprising. Thus, when tango lyrics appeared that used Lunfardo or Lunfardo-type slang, an aura of criminality was immediately added to the tango. For example, Dr. Eusebio Gomez, another criminologist, wrote in 1908 that the tango bar "was the place for obscene songs, alcohol, cheap women, and 'hot' music where innocent country boys were led astray and where young Argentines of a certain social status who could live well without working caused disturbances."[21] Gomez carried the double bias of the emerging middle class: unimpressed by the behavior of wealthy young men, yet blaming the lower class for leading them astray.

The history of Lunfardo receives a broader interpretation from later scholars, who noticed that, except for understandable words such as *mina* and *bacan,* the words quoted in Dellepiane, Lugones, and others were not those found in tango lyrics. The Lunfardo of the criminal class was essentially technical jargon for a particular profession, whereas tango lyrics were about women, sex, alcohol, good times or betrayal, and social criticism. Thus it is generally accepted that there were two branches of Lunfardo that did not merge until after 1900.[22] The criminal's Lunfardo would have had no need for the double entendres found in many tango titles and lyrics.

An example of the tango's use of Lunfardo is Angel Villoldo's "Cuerpo de alambre" (Agile Body). Villoldo was a master poet who frequently used Lunfardo. The complexity of Lunfardo becomes clear when one tries to use an ordinary Spanish/English dictionary to translate tango lyrics. To illustrate that point, both the original poem and Donald Castro's translation are included here:

> Las turras estritadoras
> Al manyarla se cabrean
> Y entre ellas secretean
> Con maliciosa intencion.
> Es mi china la mas pierna
> Pa'l tango criollo con corte;
> Su cadera es un resorte
> Ya cuando baila un motor.
> Hay que verla cuando marca
> El cuatro o la media luna,
> Con que lujo lo hace ¡ahijuna!

> Clumsy women become angry
> When they see how skilled she is.
> Jealous, and among themselves
> They gossip with malicious intent.
> My woman is the very best
> At dancing the creole tango
> With its complicated twists and turns;
> Her hips are like a coiled spring
> And when she dances she goes full tilt.
> You must see her when she twists, turns,
> And marks the complicated steps,
> And what a show she puts on
> What a fine thing she is![23]

For example, none of my several Spanish dictionaries gave any definition of *turras, estritadoras,* or *china,* or anything close enough to be a variation or different form. Even for some common words like *pierna* the definitions are not useful here. One must find a dictionary of Lunfardo or other slang to approximate the poem's meaning.

Villoldo contributed to the tango in many ways. As a master poet and superb dancer, he helped to create the new form. As a coachman and streetcar driver, he was one of many who helped to spread the tango throughout Buenos Aires. The appearance of coachmen and drivers in tango lyrics is not coincidental. Through their profession they had contact with a wide range of people, including not only the *orilleros* but also the servants of the wealthy—a group of people interested in the tango who served as another link or access point to the tango for the upper class. As a group, the drivers were often involved in radical labor politics.

Villoldo's lyrics convey many of the social issues of concern to the lower class as well as everyday themes of working-class life: "El carrero y el cochero" (The Tramway Motorman and the Coachman, 1910) and "El rey del conventillo" (The King of the Tenement House, 1913) are two of the latter. "Filo criollo" (Creole Thief, 1907) addresses men out of work because of strikes, and "Los cabreros" (The Tough Angry Ones, 1912) concerns the fear of deportation over labor activism. Many such poems and lyrics existed only in oral tradition, since their major market was among an illiterate class, and the Lunfardo required explanation when the poetry was offered in written form to those who could read.[24]

The Tango in the Theatres of Buenos Aires

Theatrical forms available to the upper and middle classes showcased aspects of the tango and the stereotypical characters of the *orilleros*. Beginning in the 1860s, Spanish *zarzuelas*[25] were popular and often included the Spanish tango *andaluz*. Vaudeville was represented in the Teatro de Revistas. The form that brought the Buenos Aires tango onto the stage most powerfully was the *sainete porteño,* a one-act burlesque or comic farce with music. Typically a large cast was involved, and many local or native actors who went on to act in legitimate theatre got their starts in the *sainetes.* These one-act shows used a great deal of physical action and comedy, and many circus performers were recruited, including circus families such as the famous Podestás. Blanca Podestá in particular went on to become a well-known tango performer, while Ricardo Podestá contributed the following tango lyric:

> y la forma de mi cuerpo
> arreglada a mi vestido
> me hace mozo muy querido
> lo juro
> lo juro por esta cruz.
> soy el taita del barrio
> preguntaseló a cualquiera.

> In my tight fitting clothes
> I am a fine figure of a man dearly loved;
> I swear it
> On this cross I swear.
> I am the boss man of the neighborhood;
> Just ask anyone.[26]

While circus performers were generally socially acceptable, actresses were not. Despite the taint on the circus when its stars left for the theatre, and the supposed links between the theatre and white slavery, these new chances at stardom proved to be a powerful attraction for young immigrant women.[27]

The *sainete* was important to the tango in several ways. Many of the plots were based on local vignettes or social themes involving *compadrito* society and the growing tensions between them and immigrants. In addition, since many tango poems were known only through oral tradition, the *sainete* contributed extensively to the preservation of early lyrics and to the understanding of Lunfardo and tango language by the middle and upper classes.

Many of the extant *sainetes* include blunt social criticism, as in this example from *Los inquilinos* (The Tenants) of 1907. This tango makes the following commentary to the character of the Lord Mayor:

Señor Intendente,
los inquilinos
se encuentran muy mal
se encuentran muy mal
pues los proprietarios
o los encargados
nos quieren ahogar.

Abajo la usura
y abajo el abuso;
Arriba el derecho
y arriba el derecho
del porbre también.

Mister Lord Mayor,
the tenants
are in a very bad state.
are in a very bad state
because the landlords
or their agents
want to smother us with their rents.

Down with unfair charges
and down with their abuses;
Up with justice
and up with justice
for the poor have rights too.[28]

One of the most widely remembered *sainetes* is *Justicia criolla,*
with words by Ezequiel Soria and music by Antonio Reynoso. First
produced at the Teatro Olimpio on September 28, 1897, it included the following dialogue:

> *Gregorio:* Let's see if we can liven up this girl!
> *A man:* A waltz!
> *Some of the crowd:* No, no—tangos!
> *Others in the crowd:* Quadrilles!
> *Benito:* Something a little calmer, boys, that everyone will be

able to dance. Like good criollos, we propose to fire up
this show with a tango, and if most of you agree, the gui-
tarists can pluck their strings.

All: Tango! Tango!

Benito (aside): How quickly they agree! I have an excellent
puppet for controlling the majority.[29]

Benito also provides the following account of how he won his
sweetheart, Juanita:

It was a Carnival Sunday
and I went dancing at the Pasatiempo.[30]
I asked Juanita to dance a Scottish [*sic*]
and I decided to draw out her love.
I poured laments into her ears,
I was so tender and talked so much
that she was moved
by my thousand promises of eternal love.
I told the broad about my courage . . .
She was silent and so I showed off prodigiously,
and then in a tango I was so skillful
that I seduced her with pure *cortes.*[31]

By the late 1800s, many of those who adopted the *compadrito*'s identity and those who were involved in the world of
the tango were people who had been born in Buenos Aires, no
matter what their distant European backgrounds might be.
Nonetheless, the tide of immigrants continued and another layer
of social tension was soon in place: that between the creole *compadrito* society and the most recent, particularly Italian, immigrants. In the streets this resulted in the *duelo criollo*—a duel between a Creole and an immigrant. These duels were highly
ritualized, and the type of knife chosen and the type of wounds in-
flicted indicated the level of respect or disrespect each fighter had
for his opponent. Eventually, the tango replaced the knife, and the
level or lack of respect was indicated by the tango's lyrics and the

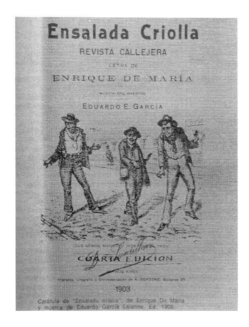

Fig. 1.3. Cover from the libretto of *Ensalada criolla*. Reproduced in Savigliano, *Tango*, 39.

complexity of tango steps. This ritualization of conflict suggests another interpretation for the phenomenon of men dancing the tango together: perhaps the tradition grew as much out of conflict resolution as out of teaching and competitive performing. Another stage work, *Ensalada criolla,* with words by Enrique de Maria and music by Eduardo Garcia Lallane, included just such a tango competition among its main characters. The "salad" in the title refers to the mix of races forced to live side by side in the poor neighborhoods, with each race keeping its own internal prejudices.[32]

Many themes, including the *duelo criollo,* are tied together in a scene from Pacheco's *Los disfazados* (The Masqueraders), a *sainete* of 1908. The following events take place: first, two Creoles argue, and one insults the other for selling out his creole heritage to the foreigners. Later, an immigrant is insulted and beaten up by a gang of creole ruffians. Finally, the immigrant kills the Creole who insulted him, thereby acting as the innocent agent of the upper classes in their plan to eliminate the Creoles.[33]

Thus, by the end of the nineteenth century the tango was highly visible to people of all classes in Buenos Aires. Bands of upper-class young men would try to gain entrance into lower-class society through the tango, and the immigrant poor both revered it as a way to be the equal of any *porteño* and feared it as a dangerous way of life for their sons and daughters. That the immigrant poor could feel the frustrations and loneliness represented by tango lyrics is no surprise. Although written somewhat later, at least one tango lyric, "La violeta," expresses the Italian connection to the concept of *mufarse:*

> Con el codo en las mesa mugrienta
> y la vista clavada en un sueno
> peinsa el tano Domingo Polenta
> en el drama de su immigración . . .
> Canzoneta del pago lejano
> ue idealiza la sucia taberna
> y que brilla en los ojos del tano
> con la perla de algun lagimon
> la aprendio cuando vino con otros
> encerrado en la panja de un buque
> y es con ella metiendo bataque
> que consuela su desilusión.

> With his elbow on the filthy table
> and his eyes fixed on a dream,
> thinks the Italian Domingo Polenta
> about the drama of his immigration.
> Song of a far away land
> that idealizes the dirty tavern
> and that shines in the eyes of the
> Italian as the pearl of a tear.
> He learned it when he arrived
> with others in the bowels of a ship
> and with it in his mind's eye
> as a consolation against his disillusionment.[34]

The Tango as a Social Dance

The stereotype of a steamy bordello filled with gangsters and ladies of easy virtue all dancing the tango as a prelude to other activities is, as far as it goes, probably accurate. However, other venues were also available, particularly after the theatres introduced the tango to the middle class. In addition to Arturo Penon's description of a courtyard dance and Batiz's description of a street dance, many dance halls, bars, and cafés sprang up that offered opportunities to encounter the tango in a variety of ways. Vicente Gesualdo lists the following among the places where women served drinks but only the men danced the tango: the Palomar, the Tancredi, "Tanto" Nani's place, the Red, Rosendo's, La Pajarera Café, and La Fazenda Bar. These places in the Palermo district were the settings for many clashes between lower-class *guapos* and upper-class young men. On the waterfront, in the area called La Boca, there were also many places where no one danced, but both men and women would gather to listen to tangos sung and performed by the latest generation of composers.[35] Luis Adolfo Sierra says that these café concerts lasted until approximately 1910.[36]

The most common venue in the early years of the tango was apparently a sort of combination establishment where one could find drinking, gambling, dancing, and dancing women, some of whom might be prostitutes. These places were variously known as *academias,* tango bars, and clubs, among other names. Often they were named for their proprietor or, especially, proprietress, if that person was a colorful local character with a distinctive reputation.

Not surprisingly, lower-class dancing establishments had always suffered the same kind of bad reputation in Argentina that they had elsewhere. On January 14, 1868, an article in *La tribuna* stated, in part, "[We called these places] Academias de bailes . . . these gatherings that happened in the streets of 25 de Mayo and

Maipu where people of the evil life gathered to dance, and where all types of scandals were seen. . . . The police nevertheless from time to time made raids in order to take some money from these places."[37] And from an editorial notice in the same newspaper, February 15, 1870: "*La Pandora*. We call the attention of the police to the dancing place known under this name. The scandals are tremendous."[38] One well-known early tango dancer, Viejo Tanguero, left some reminiscences in the magazine *Critica* in 1913.[39] He believed that the *academias* were more modern forms of the *piringundines,* traditional gathering places where the gauchos and *payadores* could meet, trade, and enjoy music, dancing, and poetry. When these people migrated to the city, their attempt to re-create their social clubs was one ingredient in the creation of the tango clubs. Dr. Veygas (perhaps Carlos Vega?), writing in 1904, also gave a fairly innocent interpretation of the *academias:* "The *Academia* was simply a café where women served [drinks] and played music, generally on the *organillo;* with these sweet stimulants [men] drank and between many glasses they danced with [these] same waitresses."[40]

That police reports are full of incidents in these and other gathering places is hardly the fault of the tango, since similar reports predate the tango's appearance and continue after its acceptance into mainstream life. Rather, as in most countries, the combination of poverty, overcrowding, alcohol, and dancing led to the bad reputation given by high society to places where poorer people were daring to have too much fun.

As the theatres brought the tango to the middle class and the upper class continued to join in the dancing, the tango was offered in higher-class establishments. The famous Hansen's in the Palermo district was one such club, and the Hotel Victoria also offered tango dancing. In addition, the reputations earned in Parisian society by the first wave of visiting Argentine composers provided an introduction into the society cafés of Buenos Aires for the tango orchestras, called *orquestas.*

The Early Tango: Its Style and Its Dancers

As anyone who has ever tried to write down dance steps knows, dance is highly subjective and difficult to describe with absolute clarity. Even so, scholars eagerly await the day when someone locates a source that describes with clarity and detail the steps of the earliest tango. Many people, however, wrote something about the style of the early dance, although even those descriptions vary greatly according to the perspective of the writer. One description is from *La nación,* September 16, 1896:

> These indecent public dances for people of color attract people uninformed about their way of life. All go to the Pasatiempo for the [risque] cinema and the unique dancers. . . . Waiters cross the salon carrying cognac, beer, and other drinks. . . . The feminine element is represented by blacks, Englishwomen (Blondes), Germans, and [others]. The men are almost all young, men of color and sons of good families. . . .
>
> The orchestra plays, the couples meet, and they dance. What do they dance? A habanera, a milonga, a polka, a mazurka. How do they dance? The *criollo* dance, purely *criollo,* advancing as is everything in this country, and those who have seen little of this dance *con corte y quiebre,* they don't understand that this is modern dancing. The basis is rhythm, the goal is love. Sensual, easy, undulating, full of surprises in the movements that accompany the syncopated music, each dancer, each couple is a picture of changing attitudes. They go too far, gyrating and doing turns . . . that can carry them to hell. . . .
>
> The wide edge of the trousers is folded at the cuff to keep the mud off the carpet while dancing, there are handkerchiefs around the necks, and the hands may or may not be used to grasp the partner. In the first case, the bodies are separated as much as possible, the hands are held tightly, with the arms extended and the rhythmic dance figures are produced. In the second case, the man has his arms crossed behind her, with his hands at waist height. The woman does the same and only the

fronts of their bodies touch. Thus the couples follow the customary dancing position, and within the large framework . . . each couple has its own style. . . . They spend each intermission passing from room to room, to the café . . . they have a drink, and return to the dance. Upon leaving, in the street, they produce the quarrels and fights that almost always end in death.[41]

Another description comes from the text attached to a series of five photographs taken in the Hotel Victoria in 1905. The text is by Goyo Cuelho, and the series is entitled *Baile de moda:*

During the Carnival, the tango is made Lord and Master of all the dance programs, and the reason is that it is the most libertine dance. Only in these days of insanity are we able to tolerate it. There is no theatre where new tangos are not announced. It is a great incentive for the dancing clientele, who are eager to show off for the *compadres* and do the fancy figures that the lascivious dance draws to itself like flies to honey.

Each show is something original; the most admirable is in the Victoria. The room fills with happy people, everywhere one hears phrases that could make a vigilante blush. In the background the group of *malevos* of the *barrios* with improvised disguises, in the theatre boxes handsome men and even more handsome girls. Suddenly, the orchestra begins with a tango, and the couples begin to form. The *chinerio* and the *compadres* join together in a fraternal embrace, and then the dance begins, in which the dancers show such art, that it is impossible to describe the contortions, dodgings, impudent steps and clicking of the heels the tango causes.

And the couples glide energetically to the beat of the dance, voluptuously, as if all their desires are placed in this dance. There in the background, the people form groups to see figures done by an *orillera,* who is proclaimed the mistress without rival in this difficult art, and the crowd applauds these prodigious figures, drawing back scandalized when the *companero* of the dancer says, "Give me the pleasure, my *china.*"

Fig. 1.4. Illustration of a tango dance from c. 1905. From the Archivo General de la Nación, Buenos Aires.

This is the most excellent dance of the outskirts. It is the reason that the *compadre* exhibits his abilities, by which he demonstrates all the agility of his body. . . . And for this it is fashionable during Carnival.[42]

Much of the creation of the tango dance grew out of the *compadrito* society's unique treatment of the polkas, mazurkas, waltzes, and quadrilles known to everyone. The goal was an exaggerated style, highly ornamented with filigrees and *refaladas* (ornamental steps) of various kinds. According to Vicente Gesualdo and others, early choreographic elements included *taconeos* (heel clicks or stamps), *corridas de costado* (side-steps), *cortes y quebradas* (stops and swaying hips), *media lunas* (steps that trace a crescent shape), and *sentadas* (steps in which the man extends his leg and the woman sits on his thigh and, possibly, kicks between his legs). Daniel Cardenas adds to this list the *doble corte* (double *corte*), *medio corte* (half *corte*), *abanico* (fan), *ocho* (figure eight), *doble ocho* (double figure eight), *alfajor* (unknown), *volteo* (turn), *marcha* (walking step), *paseo atras* (back-step), *cruzado* (cross or scissors), *corrida Garabito* (unknown, but see Batiz's memoirs above for mention of the Garabito brothers as well-known *tangueros,* or tango dancers), *cuatro* (four-unknown), *media vuelta* (half turn), *rueda* (wheel), *paseo de lado* (step to the side), and *paseo con golpe* (step with stamps).[43] Gesualdo believed that the fact that these steps were done in a highly exaggerated style by *compadritos* caused the tango to keep its sullied reputation for many years.[44] Leon Benaros adds that eventually the image of the ideal tango dancer changed from the theatrical contortionists of the early style to those who danced with a smooth, intimate seriousness.[45] This transition to a smoother style coincides somewhat with the acceptance of the tango by Buenos Aires high society, and one cannot help but compare the gradual acceptance of the one-step, foxtrot, and other such dances in the United States and Europe once dance teachers demonstrated that a smoother, more elegant style was possible.

It is tempting to impose on the list of Argentine steps the choreographies of their later European counterparts. It is also tempting to look to the modern Argentine tango, which still uses most of the same names for steps, and, combined with one's vision of *compadritos* and their exaggerated style, imagine that one could accurately re-create the very early Buenos Aires tango. Yet, in the words of Cardenas, "Logically, the passing of years was reflected in all aspects of the tango and because of that . . . a tango of 1880, played and danced according to the times, would perhaps fill us with enthusiasm or confuse us completely."[46] Dancers can of course make educated approximations, and many current stage shows make credible attempts, but until choreographic descriptions are discovered, such attempts must carry the caveat that the exact steps of the earliest tangos are still lost to us.

Just as the names of tango steps have survived, so have those of many famous tango dancers. To many Argentines they are folk heroes. Almost all of the Argentine sources consulted here list one or more famous dancers. It is interesting to note that women who danced the tango are as well remembered as men. These names are prominent: La parda (mulatta) Refucilo, Pepa la Chata, Lola la Petiza, La Mondonguito, Maria la Vasca, La china Venicia, Carmen Gomez (proprietress of a notorious establishment), La Tero, La Flora, La Fosforito, and Sarita Bicloruro, so named for the drugs she used during two suicide attempts. The male dancers had equally fanciful nicknames: El flaco (skinny) Saul, Mariano, El Civico, El Moscovita, El Mocho, El vasco (Basque) Ain,[47] El pibe David, El flaco Alfredo, Cimarra, El petizo Zabalita, and El Cachafaz. Jose Ovidio (Benito) Bianquet, El Cachafaz (The Insolent One), is perhaps the most famous of all the tango dancers. He was also one of the few among the large numbers of dancers who traveled abroad to be able to make a living full time as a *tanguero.* Between 1911 and 1919 he traveled to the United States, back to Buenos Aires to open a successful *academia,* and then on to Paris to dance at the El Garron cabaret.

After 1900 the tango was highly visible to all social classes in Buenos Aires. What remained was for it to earn acceptance as a dance representative of all Argentines, without regard to social class. Serious authors had not yet included the tango in accounts of Argentine literary, theatrical, or social history. One exception was Ernesto Quesada, professor of sociology at the University of Buenos Aires and author of books on Argentine culture. In 1902 he published *El criollismo en la literature argentina* (Nativism in Argentine Culture), in which he mentions the tango, the *sainete porteño,* the gaucho dialect, the dialect of the *orillero,* street parties for singing favorite tangos, and the spread of the tango throughout Buenos Aires by the coachmen and the servant class.[48] The upper class was divided on what to do about the tango, splitting between *tolerantes,* who wanted to allow tango dancing, and *prohibicionistas,* who wanted it outlawed. The Bunge family, distinguished members of the upper class, displayed this split in their memoirs. Julia Valentina Bunge left entertaining memoirs of life in Buenos Aires around the turn of the century, but she never mentions the tango. She must have known of it, however, because her brother, Carlos Octavio Bunge, mentions the tango in his own work, *Nuestra America.* In addition, another of the Bunge daughters was the wife of Manual Galvez, author of *Nacha Regules,* a novel set in the milieu of the tango.[49] Perhaps Julia Valentina's reluctance was gender-based: society women could still only have known of the tango by report. Only men could dare to travel to those districts where the tango was danced or afford to be seen with the *compadrito* society. The next stage of the tango must therefore be sought in the cafés and dance halls of Europe, as the tango found its way into the repertoire of new dances that swept the ballrooms of Europe and the United States in the years before World War I.

2   Europe and the United States Discover the Tango

"Emulate the sinuous grace of the tiger."
—Les Alamanos, tango dancers in Paris, 1913

The New Dances of the Ragtime Era

 By the end of the nineteenth century the ballrooms of Europe and North America had settled into an unchanging and limited repertoire of dances. Despite the efforts of dancing masters to keep the variety of dances from mid-century alive (the mazurka, schottische, and gallop are good examples of once-popular dances that had fallen out of favor), even a cursory glance at ball cards and programs from the 1880s onward reveals a tedious pattern of waltzes, two-steps, and quadrilles repeated over and over. It is no surprise, then, that the appearance of ragtime music led to the development of new kinds of dance music and dance steps. Younger dancers slipped away to dance halls and clubs where the new music was played, and a variety of dances were born, such as the one-step, the blues, the maxixe, the hesitation waltz, and the infamous "animal dances" (such as the grizzly bear, dog trot, turkey trot, and bunny hug).

The one-step was the most accessible of these and became the most popular dance of the ragtime period. Its music was lively and modern, but not necessarily syncopated like ragtime music. In the one-step, dancers took ballroom position and took one step per beat of the music, moving in a great variety of patterns on the floor. The blues used many of the same step variations as the one-step, but the music was often slower and dancing less frenetic. The maxixe was a Brazilian polka or two-step, rejected by polite society in Brazil but enjoyed by some ragtime dancers in Europe and the United States. Here dancers swayed against the direction they were stepping and used a number of graceful and characteristic arm movements. The hesitation waltz was the ragtime era's solution to increasingly fast tempi in waltz music. Instead of turning and taking a step for every beat, dancers took one step for every three beats of music. The animal dances had dancers use a variety of arm positions, often draping themselves around each other's necks in ways that many people found suggestive and obscene. The dance steps, which included different patterns of slow and quick steps with hops and kicks thrown in, were meant to depict the movements of the creatures (grizzly bears, dogs, foxes, bunnies, fish, etc.) for which the dances were named. Of this group only the foxtrot remains in the repertoire. Although few of these dances were accepted by polite society, dancers were ready for a change, especially if enthusiastic, elegant performers presented the new dances.

The most famous representatives of the new dances were Vernon and Irene Castle, a young couple who both started out in vaudeville, then had brief but meteoric careers in New York and the supper clubs of Paris. The Castles were noted for their fresh, inventive dancing, their smooth, elegant style, their extreme thinness, and their boundless energy, which allowed them to teach all day and dance most of the night. They based their enterprise in

Figure 2.1. These silhouettes of ragtime-era dancers are taken from various Argentine record labels and advertisements. They illustrate the positions of many of the most popular ragtime dance steps.

New York, attaching their names to many dance activities and places: Castle House was their studio, Castles in the Air and Castles by the Sea their dance clubs, and the "Castle House Rag" was composed for their business. There were Castle dancing shoes, Castle foot powders, and many other logos and marketing promotions using the Castles' names and pictures. Irene's clothes and daring short hair were widely copied, and her opinions on fashion and hostess duties were widely sought. Vernon's dashing style was the ideal for gentlemen who wanted to be sophisticated dancers. The Castles eschewed the rowdier animal dances and concentrated on a level of elegance and grace to which all ages could aspire. In a very few years they had amassed a great fortune. There seemed to be no end to their influence and popularity until Vernon's tragic and untimely death during training exercises for the Royal Air Corps in Texas during World War I.

The atmosphere created by the Castles and other performers of ragtime-era dances, plus the knowledge that there were additional, even more lively and sometimes forbidden dances to learn, led to an explosion of interest in social dancing, particularly when a new dance included a slightly risqué element. In other words, the time was ripe for the tango to burst onto the scene, and its transmission to Paris by young Argentine aristocrats happened at just the right moment.

The Tango Arrives in Paris

Throughout the nineteenth and early twentieth centuries, Argentine high society traditionally sent its sons to Europe to take the grand tour and do those things young men must do when they come of age. For many young Argentines this meant a great deal of time spent in the supper clubs and cabarets of the Paris demimonde, especially in Montmartre. Though they could learn nothing new about dance in society ballrooms, they found surprising developments in the lower-class clubs. The Parisian demimonde had a dance called the *Apache,* and in it the Argentines claimed to find a spirit kindred to that of their tango. A mutual exchange of steps and styles ensued, and thus the tango found its way to Paris.[1]

The term *Apaches* originally referred to gangs of sometime-criminals—male and female—in turn-of-the-century Paris.[2] Often each female *Apache* was attached to a particular male, much as a *mina* was attached to a *compadrito.* A New York newspaper clipping from 1909 provides this description:

> The Paris female *Apache* is becoming as terrible a scourge as the loathsome individual who, cap on head, hands in pockets, and armed to the teeth, lurks about the outer boulevards with the inevitable cigarette hanging from his underlip, or sits in a low café drinking his absinthe or his *petit verre.* At the Paris salon three years ago a painting excited much attention, chiefly on account of its terrible realism. It was what the Parisian call *d'actu-alite*—up to date—and represented two young women, knife in had and stripped to the waist, fighting a duel, while a couple of cynical male *Apaches* looked on. It was a definite recognition of the place the female *Apache* had won for herself in the domain of criminal life.[3]

The men described in this article clearly resemble the Argentine *compadritos.* A later paragraph describes a man and a female *Apache* named Chiffonette who resemble a *compadrito* and his *mina:*

> She . . . took atrocious revenge on her first sweetheart because he dared to deceive her. The wretched man, attacked in his sleep, was reduced by Chiffonette to such a pitiable state that he had to spend six months in a hospital. When he came out again he asked Chiffonette to marry him, vowing that if she refused he would shoot her. Chiffonette pretended to acquiesce, took the necessary steps for the banns to be published, and then, two days before the wedding, laughed in her sweetheart's face and told him she only was fooling him. The *Apache* whipped out his revolver, and fired three shots.[4]

The story increases in violence, resulting in the deaths at Chiffonette's hands of both her sweetheart and the woman she accused of betraying him to the police.

The *Apache* dance parodied the wild style adopted by these fearsome women. One of the few primary sources to describe it is the manual *Maurice's Art of Dancing*.[5] Its author, Maurice Mouvet, was second in popularity only to Vernon and Irene Castle during the ragtime dance craze, and he often appeared onstage with his partner, Florence Walton. Mouvet describes the *Apache* not with the other dances but in an aside in the brief autobiography with which he begins his book. This description is the culmination of an entertaining tale in which he is persuaded to visit some of the underground haunts in Montmartre. The dance steps themselves are of little interest to him, as the *Apache* is more of a drama than a dance. He describes the figures in this order: "1st position: He asks for money: she refuses. . . . 2d position: He threatens; she defends herself. . . . 3d position: The dance starts. . . . 4th position: He throws her to the floor, then takes her to his arms again. . . . 5th position: The walk step. . . . 6th position: The Challenge." The dance ends when the man wins both the woman and the money and goes back to his card game as though nothing had happened.[6]

A more graphic description comes from "Joe" Smith, a popular character dancer in the early 1910s:

> I was passing a café . . . at which I noticed an *Apache* woman sit down at a table and wait for some one. Soon a man appeared. I knew he asked her for money and I saw her produce it from her stocking. The man called a waiter, and ordered absinthe for both. The woman refused to drink with him. Evidently they were quarreling about another man. Suddenly he picked up her glass from the table and threw it at her, breaking it over her head. Then he rushed at her, knocking her to the ground with a vicious punch. I thought she was dead, but she calmly arose and turned her face toward him with the sweetest expression imaginable, as if imploring him for a kiss. Inside the café the

music was playing a jerky, passionate song of Montmartre. It seemed to have caught the man's ear, and he suddenly took the woman by the shoulders, drew her to him and began cavorting with her, keeping time to the music. He only cavorted; she really danced, danced with an expressiveness that I had never seen before. Not a word did she speak, but her every movement, all her grace and life, implored him to be merciful to her, to take her back and fold her in his arms.[7]

If, then, the path of transmission for the tango from Buenos Aires to Paris was indeed the mental link the upper-class Argentines made between the criminal class of Buenos Aires (only part of the group that originated the tango) and the equivalent criminal class in Paris (the originators of the *Apache*), it begins to make sense that they would introduce only the dangerous (and therefore exciting) side of the tango to European dancers. It is ironic that in tempering that image for society ballrooms, dance teachers brought the tango to a wider audience, just as it had a wider social origin in Argentina.[8]

The dancers of Paris were in just the right frame of mind to welcome the tango and share it with dancers across Europe and the United States. And this dance, more than any other of the ragtime era, divided dancers, parents, clergy, society matrons, and other guardians of public morality into groups of staunch supporters and outraged opponents.

Reactions to the Tango in Europe and the United States

All the new dances were often in the newspaper headlines, as even a quick glance at the *New York Times* indexes for 1911, 1913, and 1914 shows (see appendix 2), but the tango and the turkey trot were the most frequent targets.[9] Although the New York Public (Dance) Library at Lincoln Center almost always dates the articles in its clippings files, it sometimes omits the names of the newspapers (or cities) from which they came. As a result, many articles that clearly originate during the years under consideration, while providing a variety of opinions and anecdotal images about the tango, cannot be identified more specifically. In a 1914 article entitled "English Dancing," clearly written by an Englishman, several viewpoints about the tango are summed up at the beginning of the article, which ultimately concerns ballet:

> I am not going to say a word about the popular diversion which was described by an old lady as "one of those nasty Stock Exchange dances" (her broker must have used the term "contango" in her hearing), and has been lately condemned as "the dance of moral death" by a worthy journal written by gentlewomen for gentlewomen, presumably. . . . Truth to tell, the Tango, as danced in England by English people, is petulant rather than passionate, as mild and mellifluous as a spray of hawthorn swaying to and fro in a breeze from the West. It is not in the least like the erotic prowl *a deux* of which travelers in Spanish America (Where so many of the beautiful Spanish dances have degenerated into a kind of rhythmic bestiality) speak with bated breath. It is not even like the Tango, a strange mixture of rapture and languor, which was danced by La Guerrero at the Marigny Theatre in Paris.[10]

Even though his history is faulty, this self-admitted middle-aged Englishman who cannot dance is one of the few commentators of the time who looks at several styles of tango without praising or condemning them all of a piece.

Other articles from the London press include a notice that theatrical tragedians "would condescend to tango" at a function sponsored by the Theatrical Ladies' Guild of Charity, acknowledgment that the tango would be all the rage among young and old dancers at the ever-increasing tango teas and suppers; and, in the best tradition of the English, a brief description of a combination tango dance and fried-fish supper held outside a fish shop in the Fulham Road, with music supplied by a piano organ.[11] The tango had arrived among dancers of all economic and social classes.

Although the tango was becoming commonplace in centers

of iniquity like New York, London, and Paris, such bastions of moral rectitude as Boston were slower to embrace it. Three amusing 1914 articles picked up from wire services by New York papers show a lingering tendency to condemn it. The first, "Tango, First Offence, $50 Fine," reads:

> The [Massachusetts] Legislature is asked to stop the tango in this State by making it cost $50 for the first offence and six months in jail for the second. . . . The bills says: "Dancing at public dances, entertainments or gatherings of the so-called tango, lame duck, Argentine chicken flip, bunny hug, grizzly glide or any dance participation in which is not conducive to propriety shall be prohibited. Chiefs of police are made sole judges of whether or not the proposed law is violated.[12]

Another article about the same bill is entitled "Now It's Jail for Poor Tango—He's Not Joking, Either" and takes care to point out that Representative Sullivan, the sponsor of the bill, fathered eleven children before he reached the age of forty. To Sullivan is attributed the following enigmatic quote: "I intend to make a vigorous fight for my bill, because these animal dances have reached a point where they are offensive to public morals. The tango dancer, in my opinion, is a terpsichorean futurist."[13]

A brief article with the engaging headline "Man Killed by Tango," asserts the following: "William H. Brown lost his life as a result of dancing the tango, Judge Ely ruled in the police court today. Miss Ollie Thompson, testifying at a hearing on a charge of manslaughter brought against Daniel Spencer for having caused Brown's death, said that Brown was 'tangoing' with her, when he struck his head against a door, knocking a panel out. She showed the court how they danced, and Spencer was discharged."[14]

A balance to these views is provided by other voices, including that of the Reverend Dr. Joseph H. McMahon, who gave a lecture on "Morals vs. Art" for the Catholic Library Association at Delmonico's in New York. Dr. McMahon says, in part:

> There is a certain uproar against a certain kind of dancing;
> people are thundering against it, and rightly so, because it is in-
> decent, but it will no doubt be modified and properly toned
> down and become a proper dance. A similar outburst was
> made against the waltz a century ago. We read in the newspa-
> pers of those days that a certain woman of society was shunned
> because she had been waltzing.

The article concludes:

> Dr. McMahon scorned the individuals who attempted to set up
> standards in art or literature in place of the accepted Christian
> standards that so clearly define right and wrong. "Many people
> cannot perceive the line between morality and immorality," he
> continued. "For such a bad play, a bad book, or bad art are dan-
> gerous. These things require hard thinking, and hard thinking
> has somewhat gone out of fashion these days."[15]

As if intending to prove Dr. McMahon right, the *New York
Morning Telegraph* ran a special dispatch from a National Association of Dancing Masters conference in Cleveland that described
the grudging acceptance of tango and maxixe:

> The National Association of Dancing Masters to-day decided,
> after a discussion, to approve ten sublimated and expurgated
> tango steps as demonstrated by J. E. Miles, of the Castle Danc-
> ing School of New York, and five "soft-pedaled" maxixe steps
> shown by J. G. Keane, of Chicago.
>   The dancing masters practically had agreed that the tango
> and maxixe forms of dancing must go, but the steps demon-
> strated were tamed down sufficiently to suit the majority and so
> they were accepted.[16]

And an interesting exchange of letters to the editor took place between Vernon Castle and the Reverend Edward Mack. Castle
maintained that it wasn't the dances that were vulgar; rather, it
was the way people were dancing them that could make them
look vulgar. Therefore he was in favor of the dances themselves,
properly danced. Although Rev. Mack agreed that the dances

were not vulgar, he was not in favor of the dances themselves, since the majority of people did not dance them properly.[17]

Perhaps the good citizens of Nutley, New Jersey, had the right idea:

> All Nutley is agitated by the fact that the Fortnightly Club, in planning for the informal dance at the clubhouse which is to open the social season on October 16, has submitted the question of the tango to a referendum—shall it be under the ban or shall it not be under the ban?
>
> The question was raised by some of the older members of the club filing a protest with President William F. Fairbrother. The President and the other officers dodged the responsibility by circularizing the 150 members and putting it up to them. Thus far fifty replies have come in, and the vote is just about a tie.
>
> For the most part the older couples are against the new dances and the younger couples are for them, although it is privately admitted by the President that a few quite elderly married men are found enthusiastically endorsing the tango in all its varieties. . . .
>
> . . . Meanwhile the news of a possible tie is abroad in the village, and the adherents of both sides are out working for votes as though this were one of the most important contests in municipal history.[18]

There would be no such vote a few months later at Yale University—the dean saw to that:

> "There will not be a tango danced at the 'Prom,' " said Dean F. S. Jones of the Academic Department at Yale today. "There isn't one on the card, for I have looked it over. The boys won't dance it anyway, I'm sure. There will be too many men of good breeding there. In fact, the whole tone of the 'Prom' is against it."[19]

Given the dean's confidence in the boys of Yale, it is perhaps best not to spend too much time contemplating whether additional dancing opportunities in alternative venues were sought out after the campus event had ended.

By 1915 such articles were becoming rather scarce and included an editorial, a theatre review, a ban on the tango by the
Philadelphia Dancing Masters Association, and an attempt by the
National Association of American Masters of Dancing to promote
the waltz in place of the tango.[20] One rather juicy trial covered in
the *New York Times,* however, blamed the tango and other
dances for the downfall of young women and generated the following headlines:

"Mother Seeks to Have Eugenia Kelly Committed to an Institution
   to Protect Her from Adventurers," May 23, pt. 4, 5:5
"District Attorney's Office to Ascertain How Associates Obtained
   Money from Her, Court Refuses to Postpone Hearing," May 25,
   8:2
"Mother Drops Incorrigibility Charge When Daughter Agrees to
   Give Up Broadway Friends, As Result of Trial Woods Orders In-
   vestigation of Dancing Places," May 26, 8:2
"Investigation of 'Tango Teas' &c., Ordered by Commissioner
   Woods as a Result of Kelly Trial," May 26, 8:2
"Investigation Started Upon Complaint of Mrs. Moskowitz Under
   Lieut. Dwyer, McAneny Called Upon to Act," May 27, 11:3
"Evidence to Be Given by Mrs. Moskowitz, Who Says One Noted
   Place Will Close, New Law May Be Sought, Miss Morgan De-
   fends Strand Dances," May 28, 9:3
"Mrs. Moskowitz Wants Supervision over 'Beer Parties,' " May 29,
   20:1
"R. Barry Shows Afternoon Dances Develop New Kind of Male
   Parasite Whose Victims Are Rich Girls," May 30, pt. 5, 16
"The Latest Crusade," editorial, May 31, 6:2
"Committee Preparing Report for Commissioners Bell and
   Woods," June 3, 5:2

Even some of the more serious magazines and journals could
not stay out of the tango controversy. "The Living Age," which
provided commentary on many aspects of cultural life, was pub-

lished in Boston from 1897 to 1941 and often reprinted articles from other newspapers and journals. Not surprisingly, its anonymous 1914 article from the London *Times,* "The Cult of the Tango," was one of the strongest against the dance outside of treatises condemning all kinds of dancing. This article objected to the tango not on moral grounds but on the basis of national temperament and style. In reference to the pursuit of pleasure, the author writes:

> We believe it to be natural, and sincerely hold that what is natural cannot be evil. And yet we seem to be no nearer than twenty years ago to the understanding of what is, for ourselves, natural. We import our nature. We turn for it to the negro, the South American, the ancient Greek, the modern New Yorker. With a country densely populated by fairies and goblins and sprites and elves, we make plays and ballets out of dryads and nymphs and Olympians. With a climate all our own, we adapt our women's dresses to lands of clear air and sunshine. With a hundred dances that grew out of the English temperament, and the English soil (and dozen scholars to collect and restore them for us), we toil wearily round our ball-rooms in lumpish imitations of modes of self-expression that are not, and never can be, our own. Whether we like it or not, we are English.

His assertion that the tango is not suited to the English national style seems reasonable only if one takes on faith his description of what English people looked like when they danced it.

> After watching the tango as danced on the stage or in the ball-room, public or private, he would be a bold or a very strict-minded man who could declare that it was an immodest or an indecent dance. As danced on the stage it seems to lack swing, rhythm, fluidity. The dancers are rarely in time with the music; they never appear, as good waltzers appear, to have the music so intimately "in the blood" that the music, and not their will, is moving their bodies. They are thinking of their legs and feet; and to think of one's legs and feet is to perform physical exer-

cises, not to dance. In the ball-room, for one couple that seems to be at ease, six couples are obviously ill at ease. With bowed heads and stooping shoulders, they keep anxious eyes fixed on laborious toes. They are counting steps and reckoning figures. Of the joy of dancing—of moving rhythmically to music in perfect concord with a person of the opposite sex, with the head in air and the mind free of aught but the pleasure of music and motion—the ball-room tango-dancer patently feels nothing. So far from being indecent or immodest, the ball-room tango is ungainly, ridiculous, and dull.[21]

Literary Digest provided a venue for the letters and sermons of several Catholic and Episcopal bishops in an article entitled "Against the Tango." Apparently, Cardinal Basilio Pompili (the vicar-general of Rome) had written such a vehement letter that Pope Pius X had to tone it down before it could be published in the *Osservatore Romano.* The Holy Father agreed, however, with the sentiments expressed in that letter, and those of other cardinals and bishops. Most of the letters quoted in the article condemn all the new dances, although the tango is the only one mentioned by name. Typical are the comments of the cardinal archbishop of Paris: "We condemn the dance imported from abroad known under the name of the tango, which, by its nature, is indecent and offensive to morals, and in which Christians may not in conscience take part. It will, therefore, be the duty of confessors to take notice of this in the administration of the sacrament of penance."[22] In the same vein, the Catholic patriarch of Venice, Cardinal Aristides Cavallari, condemns the tango and advises that severe penalties be imposed upon those who refused to give up dancing it:

> Cardinal Cavallari, the successor of the present Pope as Patriarch of Venice, has issued an episcopal letter which is the most energetic of all those so far published with reference to the tango, and acquires even greater importance, as it is reported to have been inspired by the Pontiff.

The letter condemns the tango in the strongest terms, referring to it as moral turpitude, and adding:

"It is everything that can be imagined. It is revolting and disgusting. Only those persons who have lost all moral sense can endure it. It is the shame of our days. Whoever persists in it commits a sin."

The Cardinal orders all ecclesiastics to deny absolution to those who, having danced the tango, do not promise to discontinue the practice.[23]

Sadly, the good cardinal passed away later that same year. His obituary in the *New York Times* comprised four paragraphs, of which one was about his stance against the tango and two were about his campaign against current "indecent" fashions in women's clothing.[24]

Most Episcopal bishops took a more moderate tone. A Bishop Darlington's response to a London *Times* questionnaire was included in the *Literary Digest* article:

My own opinion, so far as I have been able to observe, is that the new dances are no worse than the old dances which preceded them. In fact, I think the tendency is more and more toward stately walking dances and will eventually bring back the old-time minuet, to which there could be no possible objection. The present craze for dancing which has driven out so completely the former craze for bridge-whist, is a great improvement. Gambling and drinking could be combined with bridge-whist, but they can not well be with dancing. Evil-disposed persons will make evil of anything, but the tendency of dancing in proper places and under proper chaperonage is, I think, beneficial and proper.

One of the most notable features of the quotations in "Against the Tango" is the feeling among the clergy that the tango and its companions had invaded all levels and aspects of society and, for good or ill, affected more than just behavior in the ballroom. According to a talk given at Carnegie Hall by Rabbi Wise, modern dancing is only a phase of the wide spread social deterioration which we see about us.

Nothing could be more serious to a democracy than that general lowering of standards, that wide-spread debasement of tone, the evidences of which are many and multiplying. . . .

That older people indulge in the new type of dancing excuses neither the dancing nor the fools of an older growth who suffer themselves to be enticed by its low and vulgar fascination. Modern dancing is popular, not because of its grace, but because of its appeal to our lower nature.

One Anglican who disagreed about the propriety of the tango and other modern recreations was the Reverend Canon Newboldt of St. Paul's, London:

Would indecent dances, suggestive of evil and destructive of modesty, disgrace our civilization for a moment if professed Christians were to say: "I will not allow my daughter to turn into Salome, even although Herod were to give me the half of his kingdom and admit me to the much-coveted society of a world which has persuaded itself that immodesty is artistic, and that anything is permissible in society which relieves the intolerable monotony of its pleasures."[25]

Canon Newboldt was well known in London for his outspoken sermons about the social ills of the day. While Cardinal Cavallari connected the evils of modern dance with the evils of modern dress, Canon Newboldt connected them with decadent modern literature.

Nor was the dissent confined to the ethereal realms of high-level Anglo-Catholic and Jewish clerics. Even those most faithful members of congregations, the choir, could find themselves under moral scrutiny if anyone discovered the presence of a tango enthusiast among them. Not even preeminence as a soloist was enough to save one such young woman:

Warfare on the tango took a new turn here today when Mrs. Lillian Boniface Albers, soloist of St. Paul's Methodist Episcopal

Church choir, received the alternative of giving up the dance or resigning her place in the choir. She resigned immediately.

The ultimatum of the church officials was carried to young Mrs. Albers, daughter of C. K. Boniface, a hotel owner, by the Rev. W. H. Bromley of Lexington, KY, an evangelist, who has been conducting an old-fashioned revival at St. Paul's Church nightly.

"But I don't dance the tango," Mrs. Albers warmly protested.

"What do you do then?" the evangelist demanded.

"I teach it," the soloist answered. Her resignation followed.

Evangelist Bromley in a sermon declared drink to be first and the dance next as causes of immorality.[26]

The main concerns of nearly all the anti-tango salvos launched by individual clergy were the degradation of women, the immodest and immoral behavior of women who dance, and the affect on home and society when women lose their sense of decency and propriety. Rarely is a word directed toward men who danced.

Clergy holding either a positive or negative opinion of dancing might find themselves with a divided parish, as happened at a large Brooklyn church:

A Sunday school row in the Nostrand Avenue Methodist Episcopal Church, . . . which began in a dispute over the question of laying a new carpet or a new hardwood floor, came to a head on Sunday when the Sunday School Board was ordered disbanded by the pastor, the Rev. Dr. A. F. Campbell.

The row has split the congregation into two factions, headed, respectively by the pastor and ex-State Senator Eugene M. Travis. . . .

At least forty teachers of the Sunday school have resigned, the members of six Sunday school classes have severed their connection with the church, and many others in the congregation have signified their intention of joining another church of that denomination. . . .

A petition signed by 64 Sunday school teachers and 185 adult members of the school favoring a new carpet was sent to the official board. The board ignored the petition and refused to reconsider its action. Mr. Travis appealed to the congregation in a circular letter on May 15. The letter declared that the adherents of the hardwood floor proposition favored this improvement because it would provide a good place for dancing, while the faction headed by Mr. Travis, who wanted the new carpet, was opposed to any dancing in the chapel because it "would lower the tone and respect for the place."[27]

The Tango in the Ballrooms and Onstage

Among those who took a more positive view of dancing, the tango had made inroads into ballrooms frequented by all classes of society. It was also a main reason behind the creation of a new and highly popular venue for social dancing, the *thé dansant,* or tea dance. For the truly devoted, the *thé dansant* was further focused as the tango tea. In their book, *Modern Dancing,* Vernon and Irene Castle include a chapter in which Irene gives detailed instructions for hosting a *thé dansant.* According to Mrs. Castle, the new "tea with dancing" is a wonderful replacement for the old Victorian afternoon tea with its endless gossip and all-female attendance. She recommends that the floor not be too slippery and that only so many guests be invited as can be assured adequate space for dancing. Tea, coffee, chocolate, sandwiches, cakes, rolls, a light salad, and ice cream are appropriate refreshments, with lemonade or punch available in the room where the dancing takes place. Guests should be able to devise their own schedules of watching, dancing, and eating, either at a common table or at small tables placed around the room, café style.

Mrs. Castle suggests that, instead of employing the old-style receiving line, the hostess and one or two other young ladies introduce shy dancers to one another, thus ensuring that no one remains a wallflower. If the gathering is large enough, a pair of professional dancers can be hired to perform some of the more intricate dances, or else this job can be given to some of the more skilled guests, so that they can show off the results of their practice and demonstrate the latest steps. Mrs. Castle felt that the one-step, the hesitation waltz, and the tango were the best dances for such an event, the number of tangos to be determined by how familiar the dance is to the guests.[28]

One variation of the *thé dansant,* a *dîner dansant,* was an evening event that broke up the traditional multi-course meal with sets of dancing. In addition to attending these private events, dancers could enliven their weekday afternoons by dropping in on a *thé dansant* in a restaurant or club. Particularly, the tango tea was the place to show off all the newest steps or variations that any number of questionably qualified teachers were "discovering" almost weekly.[29]

Irene was not alone in her quest to admit the new dances into the drawing rooms and other venues of society. Writing slightly earlier, London dance teacher Gladys B. Crozier praises the *thé dansant:*

> What could be pleasanter, for instance on a dull wintry afternoon, at five o'clock or so, when calls or shopping are over, than to drop in to one of the cheery little *"Thé Dansant"* clubs, which have sprung up all over the West End during the last month or two, to take one's place at a tiny table—one of the many which surround the dancing floor—set forth with the prettiest of gold and white china; to enjoy a most elaborate and delicious tea, served within a moment of one's arrival, while listening to an excellent string band playing delicious, haunting Tango airs, with an occasional waltz—for those who prefer Bostoning—or lively rag-time melody, introduced from time to time? While chatting with friends, or joining in the dance, an hour or two slips by like magic, and it is time to go; but nevermind, the club meets twice a week, at least, and many of them every day.
>
> Of the many *"Thé Dansant"* clubs which have lately been started, the Thé Dansant Club organized at the Carlton Hotel by Mrs. Carl Leyel and Mrs. Fagan, which meets on Tuesday and

Thursday afternoons from 4 to 6:30, is one of the very best, as it is quite one of the most exclusive.

Once inside its rigidly guarded portals, everything is delightful in the extreme; but the thing is to get there!

Membership is strictly limited to one hundred, subscriptions are high, and election difficult, while by a special, and, in these emancipated days, rather uncommon rule, no young girl is admitted without a chaperone. The ballroom at the Carlton, though not large, is very charming, with its decoration of ivory and dull gold, its pleasantly shaded lights, and many flowers, and it is here that the Thé Dansant Club's afternoon dances take place.

Stroud Haxton is in personal attendance with his small and specially chosen string orchestra, which proves an immense attraction both to those who dance and those who merely wish to sit and watch the dancers while chatting over tea.

Well-known people are seen on every side. The dancing enthusiasts come early, and spend the whole afternoon; others drop in for half an hour; while many of the members bring parties of young people, who seem much to enjoy the novelty of dancing in the afternoon, and seldom leave until after the last bar of music has been played.

In pleasant surrounding and amidst charming company, a delightful air of informal enjoyment prevails.[30]

The *New York Evening World* of November 19, 1913, included an interview with Mrs. E. Roscoe Mathews, a leading New York society matron, about her plans to import a teacher from Argentina for a series of private tango teas for her equals in the Four Hundred. She was very clear that her motives were altogether altruistic: "I think women who have always had everything all their lives ought to try to help a bit when hard times come. It's no more than fair. My husband down in Wall Street is doing just about as much as the rest of them are doing at present. When I brought forward my plan for the winter he was afraid I would tire myself out. But my mind was made up." Mrs. Mathews was refer-

ring to a grueling schedule of tango teas to be held at the Hotel
Vanderbilt, with admission strictly by private invitation to members of New York's finest society. Her guest list included Mrs.
William K. Vanderbilt Jr. and Mrs. William Astor Chanler as well as
those unfortunate young ladies who were not "out" and so could
not participate in public dancing. They could, however, prepare
themselves by practicing with the teacher, M. Casimir Ain, at a
cost of twenty dollars per private lesson, and rest assured that
when their debuts came, they would know the genuine Argentine
steps. Mrs. Mathews and M. Ain assured society that "the real
tango is utterly different from the tango danced here. In the real
tango there is no kicking, no violent movement. The feet never
leave the floor, but move in a curious serpentine rhythm, never
hurrying and never pausing. The dancers rest their hands lightly
on each other's shoulders, and their bodies do not touch." Providing further assurance for worried husbands and mothers, Mrs.
Mathews describes M. Ain as "small, pale, and nothing to look
at"—a clear departure from the stereotype of the seductive Argentine dancer who was imagined to be such a threat to marriage
and female purity.[31]

Still, much safer for those concerned was an event such as a
dinner dance given by society leader Mrs. Stuyvesant Fish. She
followed all the fashions for dance parties of the day. However,
"Mr. and Mrs. Vernon Castle gave an exhibition of the Innovation
Waltz. Mrs. Fish does not approve of the tango, and so arranged
to have what she considered a much more graceful and dignified
dance illustrated." While it is likely that one conservative society
lady could hardly hold back the tide of tango enthusiasm, one
should note that in addition to her dinner guests, Mrs. Fish was
able to invite an additional one hundred people for after-dinner
dancing in her home. The Innovation Waltz referred to is a style of
dancing the waltz in which the partners do not touch each other at
all, even to hold hands. To dance in this way requires a great deal
of subtle communication between partners, but, successfully

done, it is graceful and elegant, as each dancer seems to read the other's mind. It must have been quite a disappointment to Mrs. Fish when dancers quickly adapted the idea and created the Innovation Tango.[32]

In his 1934 memoir *They All Sang,* New York music publisher Edward Marks recalls several entertaining, if unattributed, anecdotes about the tango:

> Henry Blossom, librettist of *Mlle. Modiste,* broke his leg dancing the tango.
>
> Mrs. Ethel Fitch Conger also broke her leg, and planned to seek legislation against the dip.
>
> A high school student collapsed and died after dancing the tango for seven straight hours.
>
> A 102-year-old man died within a week of his first try at the tango.

Marks includes this less-than-gracious description of a tango tea from an unnamed titled Englishman:

> As far as I can see, all you have to do is grab hold of the nearest lady, be she dark, fair, gray-haired, with toupee or without; grasp her very tightly, push her shoulders down a bit, and then wriggle about as much like a slippery slush as you possibly can. [Although the events were known as tango teas, this neophyte soon observed to the waiter that the teacups were unused.] "Oh sire, we seldom serve tea," [replied] the waiter, "they wiggle much better on whiskey."[33]

Although undated and unattributed, the following newspaper clipping in the files of the New York Public Library seems to fit in with events of the ragtime years:

> One good story is going the rounds: [the] heroine is one of the leaders of high cosmopolitan society. She was in the habit of going more or less regularly to one of the best of the public dancing places, and one afternoon picked up a particularly attractive partner, a handsome man, with good manners, who

tangoed divinely. The lady was charmed, the man showed a sufficiently discreet and a sufficiently adventurous devotion, a rendezvous was made for the morrow. That night the lady dined out, and the domestic in gorgeous livery who took her cloak was the partner of the afternoon. I dare not say which dancing place it was lest all the good-looking footmen in Paris should flock there in search of "bonne fortune."[34]

From the same clippings file comes the complaint that most tango teas ran from 5:00 to 6:00, but as the Paris Opera insisted on starting *Parsifal* at 6:15, much of Paris found this to be an impossible choice. Even a ban on music in the restaurants did not help, as tango music was played in the afternoons under the guise of group lessons, or in exclusive rooms that could only be entered if one knew the correct password.[35]

In Germany, society accepted the tango, but that was no help to young military officers who wanted to dance it:

> The tango, the two-step, and the one-step have been officially forbidden by the Kaiser to all officers of the German Army and Navy when in uniform. The decree . . . reads: "Officers of the army and navy are hereby requested to dance neither the tango nor the one-step nor two-step in uniform, and to avoid families where these are danced." The Berliner *Salon* asserts that dismissal will be the punishment for infringement of this order.
>
> The Berliner *Tageblatt* learns that the Kaiser's objection to the tango and one-step is so pronounced that members of the ballet of the Royal Opera House have been warned against taking part in charity entertainments at which tango competitions are included. The Kaiser's edict, if correctly reported, will upset the arrangements of the majority of Berlin hostesses, who have accepted the tango. Some young women who were to attend a course of tango lessons with German Lieutenants were informed today that the officers had canceled the arrangement, as they had received an intimation that their efforts to learn the tango would be regarded with disfavor.[36]

A Manchester newspaper article of October 1, 1913, confirms that at least the idea of the tango tea had taken hold throughout England, although the anonymous writer admits that the British preferred their events somewhat watered down from the Paris and New York versions. And despite acceptance of the events by English society, it seemed quite important to the *New York Times* to publish the following retraction:

> Inquiries made by *The New York Times* correspondent show that Frederick Townsend Martin was somewhat mixed in his facts when he stated that there had been tango dancing at Sunderland House, the London residence of the Duchess of Marlborough.
>
> The Duchess has not given any tango party, but Mrs. John Astor has given such a party.[37]

Many people, in fact, discovered the tango on the London stage, in George Grossmith's *The Sunshine Girl.* Vernon Castle was among the male dancers who performed this tango, and the music was widely available in sheet-music form. Our Manchester writer describes a theatre in London that had been converted for tea dances. The setting is similar to others described, but there is much more on the program to soften the risqué tango, including a very gentle *Apache,* an orchestra that does not quite understand the drama of the music, and a fashion parade of the latest frocks from Paris to the music of "Waiting for the Robert E. Lee."[38]

Although many London theatres expanded on the idea of the tango tea, the award must go to the Palladium for its interesting and confusing Tango Tea Revue. According to a London theatre review of November 25, 1913:

> Dance interludes mingled with passages of melodrama and excerpts from grand opera are the latest notion, it seems, of a Tango Tea Revue. Such was the entertainment given yesterday afternoon at the Palladium, and a strange, bewildering medley it was.

As the curtain went up on the "Quay Side, Rio de Janeiro," the chief actors stepped up from the auditorium. All were examined with a view to finding an absconding bank cashier. A Jewish impresario was arrested and while he proved his innocence, the real criminal had an identification mark tattooed over, then killing the tatooer. And so the story continued, at convenient moments, in the Botanical Gardens, the Casino, and the Hotel Nationale.

In all these scenes Bifflo Bull brought on his "Wild West Opera Company." Songs and choruses of every description were sung; even Wagner figured in their repertoire. But perhaps the quaintest inclusion was "Ye Banks and Braes." The genuine ring of Burns's ballad made a more startling contrast than anything else, with the ephemeral pleasures of tinsel and paint.

Instrumental music was also a prominent feature, but tango expositions were still far from being crowded out. Miss Enid Rutherford and Mr. Lloyd Garrick, Miss Ethel Payne and Mr. Tom Seeley gave numerous versions without reckoning those of the ballet. Brazilian Maxixe, Para Slide, Amazon Hop, Arroya and Chili dances were a few in the list, which finished with the "Pampa" ensemble.

No fault could be found as to the quantity of turns supplied. Perhaps it might be said that there were too many, and that a few cuts would have been advisable. One did wish, now and again, for an interval in which to pause and recover breath.[39]

Upstart dance teachers constantly afforded new tango steps to eager students, much to the dismay of dance teachers in older, established studios who struggled to keep up and maintain control of the repertoire. In addition, though much was said about style, walking—the basic element of the tango and other ragtime-era dances—freed people from the need to master the almost balletic style of mid-nineteenth-century dances and accelerated the learning process. The couple just ahead in the ballroom was as good a source of variations for many ragtime dances as was an expensive teacher. American performers flocked to Paris to learn the newest steps and be the first to show them off in society's summer watering holes at Newport and Bar Harbor.

Such was the case with Margaret Hawkesworth and Basil Durant, who were interviewed in the *London Evening Sun* of July 9, 1914, about their plans to spend the summer demonstrating "Le dernier tango," a dance that sounds like a cross between tango and *Apache,* in that tango steps are used to act out a story similar to the usual one told in an *Apache.*[40] The performers made clear that they learned the steps of this choreography in Paris by observing actual dancers in cabarets and cafés, something more and more people felt free to do instead of looking to dance teachers. To combat this freedom and growing sense of redundancy, established dance masters either condemned the tango entirely or sought to analyze and codify it under a carefully constructed and controlled system. Unfortunately for them, many would-be teachers would spend a few months in Paris, return with the latest fashionable tango steps, and set up shop as experts. Since dancers wanted their repertoire of steps to be *au courant* more than they wanted it to be documented and correct, many of the less-qualified teachers had highly successful, albeit brief, careers. The result was that dancers were convinced that there were hundreds of tango steps and began to panic over the impossibility of learning everything they needed to know to be premier tango dancers. An undated article from the *Manchester Guardian* states: "The Tango still holds its own with its slow lilt and grace. It has, it is true, 390 different steps, and as an agitated *debutante* at a country ball remarked the other night, 'How on earth am I to know which of the 390 steps my partners will do?' "[41]

Fortunately for dance historians, the ragtime dance craze had reached such a pitch that dance masters began publishing dance manuals for the general public, much as they had during the mid-nineteenth century. Since these were meant for public consumption in the tradition of Lyceum or self-education books, they are of great help in re-creating the dances of the early 1910s. In addition to those in complete manuals, descriptions of tango steps and styles were printed in magazine articles and on sheet music. A competitive attitude was common, with many writers insisting that theirs was the only authentic version, that their steps came directly from Argentina, or that professionals performed their tango onstage. Many teachers, however, adopted a more collegial approach and participated in creating basic categories of steps as well as giving some background (often faulty) and tips on style for dancing the tango.

Dance Teachers Address the Tango's Origins

Among the authors of tango descriptions that appeared in manuals, magazines, and sheet music between 1911 and 1925, fifteen address the question of the tango's origins. J. S. Hopkins and Caroline Walker sidestep the question and simply say that the tango originated in South America.[42] F. L. Clendenen, generally useful as a compiler of everyone else's ideas, stands alone in claiming that the tango is a Mexican dance that attempts to emulate "Negroid" styles.[43] P. J. S. Richardson, an English dance master, says that the tango is actually of "Negroid" origin, derived from an objectionable dance called the *Chica*.[44] Charles D'Albert, a scholarly English writer and dance encyclopedist, places its origin in Cuba, with a subsequent path of transmission through Spain and to Argentina before European dancers discovered it.[45] Not surprisingly, Spanish writers—including Condessa Stell y Pellicer—attribute the tango's ultimate origin to Spain and even describe distinct Spanish forms that remained separate from the dance as it developed in Argentina.[46] Vernon and Irene Castle agree that Spain is the original source of the tango, but they ascribe to Argentina the style, steps, music, and history that European dancers know.[47] Among those who give sole credit to Argentina are Mouvet, the French writer de Fouquières, the German Koebner, and the Italian Pichetti.[48]

Naturally, any dance master who included a written description of the tango wanted his or her students to accept it, so many writers included assurances that the tango was suitable for the ballroom and that its toned-down style had been purged of all objectionable South American elements. Vernon Castle says that the arrival of tango marks the trend away from the animal dances and other "romps" like the polka and toward "graceful" dancing, and that hence the dance does not deserve the criticism it has received.[49] De Fouquières notes that a dance done by the *bronchos*[50] of Argentina would be unsuitable for the ballroom and that the version European dancers were learning had been modified by French dancing masters. Mouvet claims that though his tango is much more like the original than most of the ballroom versions, the charge of immorality had come from very early ways of dancing it.[51] Richardson says the early European tangos were too "theatrical" to appeal to English taste and that they only caught on after English contributions made the dance much more sophisticated.[52]

Describing the Germans' sudden discovery of and devotion to the tango in 1913, Koebner calls the dance a graceful addition after all the grotesque animal dances and the "banality" of the Boston waltzes. He predicts that the music will remain fresh because of all its variations and the tension between rhythm and melody. Koebner also describes the passionate-criminal-with-a-dagger scenario from Argentina and allows that knowledge of that scenario and the role-playing it makes possible add spice once the tango has been safely toned down for European sensitivities.[53] Bergen, another German, feels that once the protests have died down, the tango will take its place among ballroom dances for connoisseurs, while Clendenen says that the combination of the tango with the habanera, a polite dance from Spanish café life, has made the tango acceptable.[54] Pichetti traces the style from lower-class Argentina to upper-class Paris and from there to both upper-class Argentina and lower-class Montmartre. Only the "obscene" versions danced in Montmartre can be considered objectionable, he says; finer society danced the tango in evening clothes in the great salons and hotels.[55]

Although writers differed slightly in their descriptions of the tango, almost all agreed that a smooth, slow gliding style was essential. It was generally the nondancing moralists, particularly those who objected to all close embraces on the dance floor, who saw the dance as sensuous and predatory. Vernon Castle, at the insistence of society leader Mrs. Stuyvesant Fish, created the Innovation Tango, in which dancers could do almost all the already-existing steps facing one another or in promenade position, but never touching their partners. Pictures of Vernon dancing in the Innovation style show him with hands in pockets, looking quite debonair.[56] But both Hopkins and Mouvet write that the lady should not be held tightly, and Mouvet also says that the dance is "centered in the knees" and that the dancers should be relaxed.[57] The Castles also emphasize gracefulness in both the hold and the smooth, gliding style of stepping.

Hopkins specifically identifies the "brushing or sweeping of the floor" as the real tango step, so that not only the bodies appear to glide but the feet remain as close to the floor as possible at all times.[58] De Fouquières says that this "tango walk" affects the way ladies walk every day,[59] and several other writers state that the characteristic way of moving smoothly and slowly is more important than the number of steps dancers know. Bergen stands alone in claiming that one distinctive feature of the tango was that a dancer did not necessarily do the same step his or her partner was doing at any given moment.[60] Although this observation disagrees with other descriptions of the dance (except for mention of a few accent kicks done by one partner or the other), the tango would not have been the first dance in which partners' steps differed. Such differences are not uncommon in Renaissance choreographies, and even some late-nineteenth-century polka variations include this feature. Bergen does not specify the source of his observation, but he might have been describing what he saw in German cabarets when two tango dancers did not know the same repertoire of steps.

Like the debutante who bemoaned her ignorance of all 390 tango steps, many dancers, reporters, and teachers were overwhelmed by the ever-increasing number of dance steps attributed to the tango. Caroline Walker of Chicago went so far as to choreograph a "One-Step Tango."[61] This was certainly in keeping with the ragtime practice of learning a step and then fitting it to a variety of musical styles and tempi: one-steps, foxtrots, and hesitation waltzes used many of the same steps, so why could the tango not follow suit? Walker cautioned dancers that the real Argentine tango was both slower and more difficult than her one-step version. Many teachers, including the Castles, spoke out for standardization of steps.[62]

Categories of Tango Steps

Maurice Mouvet, who claimed to have brought the tango to the European ballroom, said that there were about twenty authentic tango figures, of which only eight were truly well known and common.[63] Almost all the steps described in dance manuals, sheet music, magazine articles, and other sources between 1911 and 1925 fit into one of eight categories.

1. The *corte* is almost always a finishing gesture at the end of a phrase or series of steps. Most often in the rhythm quick-quick-slow, it ends in a dramatic pose with the dancers in ballroom position (face to face with his right arm around her waist, her left hand on his right shoulder, and holding her right hand in his left), the man stepping back with one foot and shifting his weight onto that foot, and the woman stepping forward with the opposite foot and leaning her weight forward. It can be reversed with the man stepping forward and the woman back. In either case, the effect is that the man draws the woman into the *corte,* with a hint of dominance beyond that of the usual lead-and-follow relationship.

Tango

Figure 2.2. Two views of a *corte*. From F. W. Koebner, *Tanz Brevier* (Berlin: Verlag Dr. Eysler, 1913), 49.

2. The *paseo* best shows the sinuous, stalking motion that tango dancers are meant to achieve. It is a slow walk, backing the lady in ballroom position, taking one step for every two slow beats, or one step for every complete habanera pattern. Most tango descriptions include the *paseo* as a step but do not include it in sample choreographies or routines. This has led some dance historians to wonder if it was a practice step, used to help dancers learn the style required but too slow for European tastes to be used as a real ballroom step.

3. *La marcha* is like the *paseo,* except that the dancers take two steps for every complete habanera pattern, effectively doubling the speed of the *paseo.* This is the most common step for beginning a tango routine in the samples given by many dance

a.   b.

Figure 2.3. Two basic dance positions: (a) ballroom and (b) promenade. From Vernon and Irene Castle, *Modern Dancing* (New York: Harper and Brothers, 1914), 42, 90.

manuals. It allows the dancers to adapt to the rhythm and tempo of the music, as well as the length of each other's stride, and to display their style and set up any role-playing games they might wish to include. *La marcha* could be done either backing the lady in ballroom position or in promenade position, with dancers side by side, both facing in line of direction with the hands held as in ballroom position.

4. *Ochos,* or figure eights, are done by making various patterns of side and cross steps in any number of rhythms. Sometimes similar steps were called scissors, and some manuals include a step called *ocho* and a different, though related, step

Figure 2.4. Beginning a scissors step. Castle and Castle, *Modern Dancing*, 97.

called scissors. The distinctive feature in each case is the tracing of a figure eight, whether open or highly compressed, on the floor. One *ocho* that survives today is done as a solo by the woman, balancing by holding only the man's left hand in her right and stepping across herself as she slowly moves toward him.

5. Grapevines are similar to *ochos* in that they involve cross steps. A grapevine does not require that dancers trace a figure-eight pattern, and it can progress in only one direction. A typical grapevine has the dancers step to the side with one foot, then cross the other foot in front or behind. This process is repeated (side-cross, side-cross, etc.), usually alternating crossing in front and behind. Partners usually cross opposite one another, although each could cross in front and then behind at the same time as the other. Grapevines are also extremely common in one-steps and foxtrots.

Figure 2.5. Beginning a *rueda.* Castle and
Castle, *Modern Dancing,* 98.

6. *Ruedas* and circles are frequently included in tango descriptions, especially where the drama of close eye contact between the partners is desired. Partners can circle each other in a
variety of ways. One common way uses Yale position, in which
partners stand with either their right or left shoulders together,
and hands held in ballroom position. Dancers can take four or
eight steps forward around each other, then reverse to touch the
other shoulder and take four or eight more steps. The *rueda* is a
special circle step in which the man crosses one foot tightly over
the other and rises up on his toes. The woman, held in a loose
ballroom position, walks around the man, turning him as she
goes, and effectively unwinds him. The *ruedas,* which require absolute balance between partners, often end with a *corte* and make
larger finishing gestures for phrases.

7. The *media luna* is unique to the tango, and some writers,
such as Hopkins, even say it is the "real" tango step. It is the step
teachers describe as "polishing, or sweeping, the floor."[64] The
shape of the step is a half moon or crescent. A typical *media luna*
would have the dancers in promenade position, both walking for-

Figure 2.6. Halfway through a *media luna*. One must imagine Irene's right foot and Vernon's left foot in motion, tracing the crescent path. Castle and Castle, *Modern Dancing,* 95.

ward and starting on opposite feet. At some point, when the outside feet were free, they would stop and each would sweep the outside foot forward in an arc until it met the outside foot of the partner. Then they would reverse the arc to the outside and step through to continue their promenade. The feet always remained in contact with the floor and enacted the sensuous polishing motion. Another example of a *media luna* is actually half a box step, in which dancers face each other in ballroom position and step backing the lady (slow), then step to the side and close the free foot (quick, quick). This pattern also frequently ends with a *corte* and was another expanded ending gesture.

8. The *molinette,* or windmill, occurs less frequently but is a distinct step. In ballroom position, the couple simply steps forward and backward, turning slightly as they do so. This step also remains in the modern repertoire, with added kicks between the partner's legs that hook the free foot behind the partner's knee.

There are some unusual steps that do not fit these general categories. In the nineteenth century these would have been called "promiscuous figures."

A special case among ragtime dance manuals that include the tango is found in S. Beach Chester's *Secrets of the Tango.* Chester claims to have constructed the book from material learned through interviews with an Argentine dance teacher working in London. This Argentine, identified as Señor Juan Barrassa, had come to London around the turn of the century to study and work as an engineer. He found, however, that he could make a great deal more money by teaching and performing the tango. Barrassa's steps, as described in Chester's manual, are certainly unique, although one could argue that they are a hybrid of an Argentine style, with heel flicks and dramatic gestures, and the European concern with even phrases and steps that work out neatly in four, eight, or sixteen slow counts of music, or two, four, or eight bars. Despite Chester's claim that Barrassa was a famous dancer among cabaret and theatre audiences in London, research into London theatre archives has not turned up a single reference to him, although programs do contain the names of other famous tango dancers mentioned in some of the dance manuals. A more detailed look at Barrassa's steps in comparison to extant Argentine sources follows in chapter 3, and descriptions of Barrassa's steps appear in appendix 1.

Appendix 1 also gives a description of all steps included in the dance manuals consulted. The following chart, organized by country and year, shows how many versions of steps in each category each dance manual describes, with one "X" for each example.

Distribution of Common Tango Steps among Dance Manuals

	Corte	Paseo	Marcha	Ocho/Scissors	Grapevine	Rueda/Circle	Media Luna/Box	Molinette	Promiscuous
U.S.A.									
Sheafe, 1913									XX
Castle and Castle, 1914	X			X		XXX	X		XX
Clendenen, 1914	XXX XXX XXX XXX XXX	XXX X	XXX	XXXXXXXX XXXXXX	XXXXX	XXXXXXX	XXXXXXXX	XXX	XXXXXXX
Hopkins, 1914	X		XXXXX X		XXXX	XXXXX	XXX		XXXXXXXX
Miller, 1914	X	XX			X	X			
Mouvet, 1914	X	X	X	X		XX	XX		X
Newman, 1914	X	X	XX	XX			X		XXXXX
Walker, 1914	XX		XX	XXX	XXX	XX			XXXXXX
Mouvet, 1915	XX		XXX	X			X		XX
Cruz, 1925			X		X	X			X
U.K.									
Humphrey, 1911	XX	X		X	X	X		X	X
Raymond, 1912	XX	X		XX		X			
de Fouquières, 1913	X	X		X		X			XXXX
Robert, M., 1913	XXX			XX		XXX	X		X
Anon., 1913	XX	X	X			X	X		
Chester, 1914	XXX	X		XXXX	X	XX	X		

Distribution of Common Tango Steps among Dance Manuals

	Corte	Paseo	Marcha	Ocho/Scissors	Grapevine	Rueda/Circle	Media Luna/Box	Mollinette	Promiscuous
D'Albert, 1914	XX	X	X	XXX	X	X	XX	X	X
Richardson, 1914	XXX	XXX	XXX	XXXXXXXX	X	XXXX	XXXXXX		XXXXXXX
	XXX	X		XXX					
	XX								
Swepstone, 1914		XX		X	XX	X	XX	X	XXXXXXX
FRANCE									
Robert, L., 1911	X		X	XXXX		X	XX	X	X
Bacton, 1912	XX	X	X	XXX		X	XXX	X	
Minchin, 1912	X	X		XX	XX		X		
Rivera, 1913	XX		X		X	X	XX		XXX
Bayo & Chrysis, 1914	X		X	XX		X	X		XX
Anon., 1920s	X			XXXX			XXX		
Anon., 1920	XXX		X	XX			X		X
Anon., 1920	XX	X	X	XXX	X	XXX	X		XX
Charles, 1920s	XXX	X	X		XXXXXX	XXXXXXX	XXXXXXXX		XXXXXXX
					X				
Peters, 1920s	XXX	XXX	XXXX	XXXXX	X	XXX	XXXXXX	XXXX	X
	X	X							
GERMANY									
Koebner, 1913	X			XX		X			
Steinke, 1914	X			XX		XX			XXXX
Bergen, 1915	XX		X	X	X	X	X		
ITALY & SPAIN									
Pichetti, 1914	X	X		XXXXX		XX	XX	X	XX
Stell y Pellicer, 1915	X			X		X	X		XX

3 Argentina Reclaims Its Native Dance

It must be a pretty dance, but it is not a tango.
—Author's 1991 interview with an Argentine *tanguera*

"Together with the girl, and it does not matter who she is, a man
remembers the bitter moments of his life, and he, she and all
who are dancing contemplate a universal emotion." . . .
"I do not like the woman to talk to me while I dance tango.
And if she speaks I do not answer. Only when she says to
me, 'Omar, I am speaking.' I answer, 'And I, I am dancing.'"
—Julie M. Taylor, "Tango: Theme of Class and Nation,"
quoting field interviews conducted in Argentina

 The Argentine response to the enthusiasm with which dancers in Europe and
the United States adopted the tango
took two forms. First, as Argentines
became aware of the changes and adaptations made to their native dance, there was a wave of nationalistic pride in preserving
the authentic Argentine version of the dance. Even today, many
Argentines discount any but the modern Argentine tango and
imply that there is something subtle, intrinsic, and noble about
the dance that only a true *porteño* can understand or portray.
Many of us who are not of Argentine descent yet try our best at
the modern Argentine tango are tempted to agree. Second, the
tango gained wide acceptance among all classes of Argentine society. It is not surprising that a high society made up of people
whose ancestors were European immigrants, and who distin-

guished themselves from lower classes by trying to be as Europeanized as possible, would wait for foreign approval of the tango
by persons of their own social class before accepting its repatria-
tion to Buenos Aires.

When the tango first arrived in Paris, men of the Argentine
upper class offered both views as to its propriety. As discussed in
chapter 2, proponents of the tango were upper-class young men
who went slumming in Montmartre and found (or created) the
connection between the tango and the *Apache.* At the same time,
warnings about the tango's scandalous origins were heard from
the Argentine diplomatic corps. When asked why the tango was
forbidden at the Argentine Embassy, Enrique Rodriguez Larreta,
the minister plenipotentiary to Paris, replied: "The tango is in
Buenos Aires a primitive dance of houses of ill repute and of the
lowest kind of dives. It is never danced in polite society nor among
persons of breeding. To Argentine ears it awakens the most dis-
agreeable feelings. I see no difference whatsoever between the
tango that is danced in elegant Parisian dance halls and that which
is danced in the basest nightspots in Buenos Aires." Other diplomats agreed, warning the women of Parisian society that by dancing the tango they were behaving like prostitutes.[1] The dancers of
Paris, however, were eager for new experiences and were just as
fond of slumming as the young Argentine aristocrats who were
teaching them the tango. That the tango came to symbolize Argentina in the decade before World War I was an additional thorn
in the side of upper-class diplomats in Paris and anti-tango moralists in Buenos Aires. The Argentine image abroad was the subject
of a special Christmas issue of *El diario* in December 1912:

> When we were all almost convinced that Europe was no longer
> considering us as "savage" and that in the old continent our
> wheat, corn, and the frozen meats were undisputed proofs and
> the best examples of our civilization and astonishing progress,
> we received—several years ago by now—the unexpected news
> that in Paris they were suddenly aware of our existence, not

through the valuable products of our soil . . . but through the
tango. . . . Moreover, it cannot be superfluous to make here an
important remark: the tango, as it is danced in Paris, has little to
do with ours except for the name and the music.[2]

The insistence that the tango was a matter of national pride,
along with demonstrations of the dance put on for the benefit of
porteño high society in venues to which they could not object,
added the final necessary element for the tango's acceptance by
Buenos Aires society. Leon Benaros offers the following example:

> In 1912, Baron DeMarchi organized a famous "fiesta" in the
> Palais de Glace, to see if *porteño* society would accept the
> tango. "Maco" Milani and Carlos Herrera were the bridge be-
> tween the forbidden tango and the honorable people on whose
> doors it knocked. The ambassadors were skillful and subtle and
> also articulate, in order to achieve their objectives.
>
> *Porteño* society, divided before, completely opened its
> doors to the tango.[3]

Thus one of the most interesting questions that arises in tracing the history of the tango can be stated simply: Whose tango is
it? Evidence shows that as soon as the dance spread from Argentina to Europe it took on new characteristics through the typical evolution of social dances, through international efforts to con-
ceal aspects of the dance some considered objectionable, and
through efforts to develop stage exhibitions. Few descriptions of
the tango exist from its early years around 1900. We have many
sources for the language, texts, and cultural importance of the
early tango; we have the music; we have an increasingly accurate
picture of where it was danced and by whom. Historians examine
the myths and commonly held beliefs about the tango's origins,
expanding areas of examination to include a larger segment of
the poorer classes of Buenos Aires and reinterpreting in particular
the roles and images traditionally assigned to women in the history of the dance.

What is missing in the reconstruction of the early tango of Argentina is primary source material about the dance steps themselves—the elusive source that says, "On count one, put your left foot *here.*" The tango existed mainly in a social class of Buenos Aires that did not write about its daily life, and nothing resembling the American and European everyman's dance manual with instructions seems to have been common for the tango in Argentina. Nonetheless, another primary source from 1914 expands on the Argentine reaction to European versions of the tango and briefly describes some basic steps as they were done in Argentina in that year. Comparing the information in that source with the tango described by "Juan Barrassa," an Argentine quoted or created by S. Beach Chester in the English dance manual mentioned in the previous chapter, is intriguing.

The Argentine source is an article in the periodical *Fray Mocho: Seminario festivo, literario, artistico y de actualidades* (Weekly Magazine of Humorous, Literary, Artistic, and Current Events), published in Buenos Aires on February 13, 1914. The article is entitled "Como se baile el tango en Argentina" (How the Tango Is Danced in Argentina). Its author, who identifies himself only as "Fritz," laments the infection of European tango-mania in even the respectable foreign journals of the day, which he says have begun to replace their customary chess problems and riddles with equally incomprehensible descriptions of tango steps. And this, according to the protesting Argentine, is only the beginning of the problem. The greater evil, as he sees it, is that Argentine journals have not leaped into battle to argue against the "absolute nonsense" European dance manuals offer as the genuine tango. In bygone years, even those Argentines who had never danced the tango and knew nothing of its steps would prefer to claim lameness rather than admit ignorance of this national treasure. But by 1914 our author takes Argentines and their press to task for a woeful lack of national pride, patriotism, and fighting spirit. Fray Mocho was also the pen name of social critic and humorist José Alvirez in turn-of-the-century Argentina, and indeed much of the moral outrage of the article under discussion here might be taken as tongue in cheek, despite the serious argument that Argentines needed to reclaim their own tango from the Europeans.

One of Fritz's protests against European versions of the tango is that they have complicated the dance out of proportion to its original simplicity and exaggerated it so much that the result is a new and different dance. Another is that the French in particular insist that the origins of the dance are to be sought entirely in earlier dances of Andalusia or Africa. Our author raises a great protest that the tango had the same origins as anything or anyone else truly Argentine—a little of this and that mixing together to form something uniquely its own. He expects that if the tango continues to be analyzed by the French intellectuals, it will soon be discovered that it is "more French than the Marseillaise . . . and that Mazarin and Queen Anne had danced it!" That would have been quite an accomplishment, since they both lived in the mid-seventeenth century.

In the hope that Europeans will correct their basic ideas of what the tango was about, but with little hope that it might actually happen, the *Fray Mocho* article offers several typical steps as they were done in Argentina that year, illustrated photographically and in diagrams by the famous dancer Francisco Ducasse and the distinguished actress Blanca Podestá. Ducasse had danced in Paris and won contests there; Podestá was a celebrity from a well-known family of circus performers and actors in Argentina. Ducasse and Podestá illustrate five tango steps whose names may be recognizable to dancers today: *paso doble, la salida, molinete, la sentada,* and the *doble sentada de vaiven.*

The source that makes an interesting comparison with Fritz's tango steps is the 1914 English dance manual *Secrets of the Tango,* by S. Beach Chester. This small book, devoted exclusively to tango dancing, provides historians with several curious riddles.

Who was S. Beach Chester? The author's gender is never made clear via any given name, although many who have read the book intuitively agree that Chester's interest in providing excessive details about corsets, dress, and manners indicates a probable female perspective. The interesting point of *Secrets of the Tango* is that Chester claims as his or her source a particular dancer from Argentina. This dancer, "Juan Barrassa," supposedly came to London through Paris, was educated in Argentina as a civil engineer and was pursuing further engineering studies. He found he could make more money as a dancer and dance teacher in London and so followed that profession instead, dancing at the Queen's Theatre. While reading Chester's dance manual, I began to have an instinctive feeling that Juan Barrassa never actually existed, and I admit to being alone in this supposition.

Requests to more than thirty theatres, archives, and libraries in London for archive searches to determine whether any concrete evidence of Juan Barrassa exists turned up no mention of him in programs, flyers, cast lists, and so forth. Many, however had notices of Marquise, another dancer briefly mentioned in Chester's book. Interestingly, Marquise and Barrassa are always two distinct personalities in Chester's book, and while the author provides no real name for Marquise, he or she does say that Barrassa used another name in private life. Raising further suspicion, Chester only describes performances by Marquise, and only Marquise is mentioned in the theater advertisements reproduced in the book. Although such negative evidence is inconclusive, one must entertain the possibility that Juan Barrassa was a composite of any number of Argentine dancers Chester might have met in those years in London.

This in no way negates the value of Chester's account of the tango in London at that time, but it does put a different slant on the information provided. If Barrassa was a composite, then Chester had to make, compile, and edit choices of what steps to include, and we must take his or her word for their being authentically Argentine, or be on guard against author's bias. Other points against the existence of Barrassa are the statements attributed to him that the old *milonga* later became the tango and that the tango had its origins among the *gauchos* of the Argentine country-side. While this misunderstanding persists to this day outside Argentina, it does not occur in any known primary Argentine source material from the years around 1914. In fact, even such European dance masters as Pichetti (an Italian who had studied and taught in Buenos Aires) were correcting it in their dance manuals.

Despite these yellow caution flags, Chester's account of the tango shows awareness of its progression through Paris, of the difference between stage and ballroom tangos, and of the controversies surrounding the authenticity of the many versions and the question of the dance's immorality. Chester cites many sources, articles, and interviews that give timely opinions on the tango and the furor created by its appearance in the ballrooms of Europe. One cannot disregard the steps Chester includes, and no doubt they did appear in studios and ballrooms and onstage. It is only when the information is attributed without question to an Argentine expert who might not have existed that Chester's book becomes far more reliable as an English-influenced source—and far less so as a pure Argentine account.

So, do both of these sources describe legitimate tangos? In all likelihood, there will never be complete agreement. Fritz's protests are alive and well even to this day. But from a historian's perspective, all the different version of the dance—Argentine, French, British, and other—make up the complex fabric of a dance that has many different forms even today. What is interesting is to compare different versions, noting where they overlap and where they diverge, as we can do for these two versions from 1914— one English, the other Argentine.

Fritz, with the help of Ducasse and Podestá, offers five tango steps. None involves more than one or two gestures, and the impression is that either the Argentine dance was made up of a succession of very small figures, repeated a number of times or combined with others into larger units, or that these five steps merely show how to begin a longer step.

In fact, three of these five steps seem to be variations on the type of *corte* in which one partner steps back and the other steps directly forward. In the *paso doble* the man makes a double gesture, passing his right leg behind the left in a curve before taking a step backward on his left. The woman makes a corresponding two-part step forward on her right foot. In *la sentada* the man does a step forward, and the woman steps back. The distinctive feature of this step is that the dancers move their feet along a curving line or path. The curve for the man is smaller, as the leg that moves is near his partner; the woman's curving gesture is much longer and wider, because her moving leg is on the outside, away from her partner. In the last of the *corte*-style figures, the *doble sentada de vaiven,* the man steps back, placing his right foot exactly in line behind his left. The woman steps forward, placing her left foot even with the man's left foot.

Fritz's *molinete* step is the only one of the five to mention a turn by the dancers. Again, the man tucks his right foot behind his left. The woman steps back on her left foot, and both dancers are told to turn. *La salida* appears to be a traveling step in which the man advances beginning with his left foot and the woman retreats, beginning with her right foot.

Although the dancers' positions relative to one another are never specifically described, the photographs of Ducasse and Podestá are in closed-couple waltz position. It is frustrating that Fritz gives no advice about how to link steps together, nor does he say whether the dancers take their steps at the same time or one after the other. He does not say if these steps are complete—not just beginnings or endings—nor does he give any idea of the timing of slow and quick beats. Dancers of the modern Argentine tango use more of the melodic phrasing to construct their dances rather than being strictly attached to rhythmic patterns and repeating phrase lengths. Perhaps this was the case in Argentina in 1914 as well, or perhaps the author felt that everyone would know what to do and that he need not include the information. The omission makes the task of reconstruction all the more difficult.

There is another small point about Fritz's photographs that is fascinating yet nearly impossible to prove. The dancers' positions in two of them seem to relate to two of the photographs in that now-famous series of men dancing the tango together. It is, of course, impossible to say how the male couple's steps were derived, but it is interesting to note that after some fifteen years, at least two of the same characteristic positions were thought to be illustrative of the tango's substance and style.

Before comparing Fritz's steps directly to those of Juan Barrassa, it is useful to consider them in the light of the catalog of mainstream European steps familiar to many fans of ragtime-era dances. For example, Fritz's *molinete* step appears somewhat similar to the *rueda* step in which the man crosses his legs and pivots to turn. The difference is that the woman steps backward as she turns instead of going forward around the man, and so she is unable to complete the *rueda*. Nonetheless, the two steps share a common shape, and it is tempting to imagine some connection. Also, it was fairly common for European and American descriptions of tango steps to include a walking step much like Fritz's *salida*. Similarities between Fritz's steps and various kinds of *cortes* have already been shown.

Barrassa includes ten steps and two variations, which differ considerably in length and complexity. Several aspects of these steps make an interesting comparison with Fritz's. Both include a walking step (Fritz's *salida*). "Barrassa" calls his *el paseo* and includes in it a *corte* in which the man steps backward. He also says that the *corte* part can be repeated several times. Another aspect of Barrassa's steps is interesting in the light of Fritz's commentary. Barrassa has the dancers execute small flourishes, kicking back or to the side before taking the final step of the *corte*. These flourishes appear in several of Barrassa's steps and may derive from the London stage. They might also be part of the exaggerated style to which Fritz objected. Yet Barrassa also objected to the exaggerations in the theatres and promoted the steps he described as the real ballroom style.

All of Barrassa's steps describe a minimum of four gestures; Fritz's give a maximum of two. It is possible that Fritz only wanted to get dancers off to a good start, without establishing long patterns, while Barrassa wanted to explain the whole thing. Yet it is unclear why Fritz does not give more information or more complete steps. Many of Barrassa's steps move in some kind of line; arbitrary experimental linking of Fritz's steps tends to keep the dancers in a fairly small area unless the walking step is used in between to cover distance. While both dances are recognizable as tangos, one cannot help but wonder what each author would have thought of the other's work.

A single Argentine source that describes only five steps is clearly not enough to unravel the mystery of how the tango was danced in its early years in Argentina. Fortunately, another source came to light some years ago, adding significantly to both our store of knowledge and our cache of questions. This source, entitled *El tango argentino de salón,* by Nicanor Lima, is variously dated 1914 or 1916. This two-year variation is a small span of time in the tango's lifetime in Argentina, but remember that the ragtime dance craze in Europe and the United States burned hot in the years before World War I, and a great deal happened between 1912 and 1916. The structure of Lima's manual is fascinating, as much for what seems odd about it as for the treasure of information it reveals. Lima includes sections on etiquette and manners, on dance history, and on appropriate dress. His step descriptions are detailed and technical, and they include the "follow the dancing feet" floor diagrams that appear in other dance manuals of the same era. The interesting point here is that this sort of detailed treatise on a social dance form does not seem to be the norm in Argentina. Argentines had been importing dances, dance teachers, and fashions from the ballrooms of Europe for more than a century. But Lima's treatise seems unique among those of Argentine authors. This begs the question of Lima's familiarity with the many dance manuals written abroad that included sections on the tango.

Of course, the biggest area of curiosity sparked by Lima's treatise is how his tango steps compare with those of the European and North American manuals. Professor Richard Powers of the Stanford University Dance Department has done considerable analysis and comparison of Lima's steps. He feels that Lima's work comprises about 50 figures and 125 variations, all of which Lima says should be done in all three basic dance positions: basic ballroom, promenade, and side by side. What might at first seem astounding is that (by comparing his reconstructions of Lima's tangos) Professor Powers has found all of Lima's steps in the European and U.S. dance manuals. Lima gives his steps names that are still familiar to many tango dancers: *pasos, saltitos, cruces, molinetes,* and *media lunas,* to name just a few. It would be so easy, and so very very tempting, to conclude that Lima has established a core similarity between the early Argentine tango and the ballroom tango of Europe and the United States. Easy and tempting, but quite premature, as questions arise almost immediately. Why was such a dance manual not produced in Argentina before 1914/1916? And if it wasn't needed before, why was it needed then?

Lima's book was written during the years when great efforts were made to get Argentine high society and guardians of morality to accept the tango and to reestablish claim to it as an icon of Argentina. It was also a time when many Argentines had traveled to Paris and London and experienced their foreign peers enjoying and accepting the tango. Thus one of the more frequent arguments advanced to Argentine society was that the foreign society they strove so hard to emulate had already accepted the dance and that they must as well, in order to remain *au courant.* Paris had never lost its influence on the Argentine sense of style.

So, who was the intended audience for Lima's book? The book itself gives several clues, beginning with the title. Lima writes about the Argentine tango "of the salon" or parlor. He wants his tango admitted to the drawing rooms and clubs of polite society. Another clue is the structure of the book. As noted, Lima includes etiquette and technical aspects of dancing that most likely would not have been needed by those whose tango traditions were unbroken. But the tango was rather new to the conservative element in society, which would have wanted to know the "proper" way to do things.

Then there is the question of the steps themselves. During the years around 1914, when Argentines were well aware of how Europeans and Americans were dancing the tango, there were many protests about how the tango was being changed and how Argentina should once again establish itself as owner of the only true tango. Lima joins in these protests:

> It is necessary to put things in their place, and consequently, to tell Europe what our true tango is. It is the case in the other hemisphere, and even in our own country, that in our efforts to create diverse steps, many have applied to our beautiful dance every capricious, silly little thing imaginable, making the dance ridiculous.
>
> It is this circumstance that led me to write this book, to spread the knowledge of the true Argentine Tango, the one and only, and to point out that there is no "Parisian tango," and if there were, it would only be a degenerate copy of the Argentine Tango.[4]

But if that is the case, why are Lima's steps the same as those found in European dance manuals? It may be that Lima is speaking out against those things in European dance manuals that he does not include in his own. According to Professor Powers, Lima ignores such things as the exaggerated dips found in many rag-time dances as well as the fanciful steps and sequences created for stage shows. Also, Lima makes a particular point of snubbing Vernon Castle's Innovation tango (in which dancers mirror each other but never touch) by saying there is never a point in the real tango when the dancers let go of one another.

Still, one cannot avoid the reality that Lima's book appeared after the tango had traveled across the Atlantic and returned home. And this, coupled with all the layers of protests about the tango in Argentina (high society vs. lower classes, elegant dance vs. vulgar dance, salon vs. dance hall), highlights again the question of what Lima was trying to achieve with his book. It may be that the Europeans and North Americans got it right to a greater degree than we have customarily credited them in their efforts to dance real tangos. But it may also be that Lima wanted a stamp of legitimacy for the tango among those whose opinions mattered in shaping the culture of Argentine society. Either way, it is important not to jump to easy, attractive conclusions that might be hard to put aside. And, although 1914/1916 is much closer to the earliest tango than we are today, Lima does not prove to us how the tango was danced around 1900, before changes had been made. It seems we may have to live with Lima's book a while longer before drawing definitive conclusions.

Many scholars agree that the tango was accepted by all of Buenos Aires (except for those who disapproved of all dancing) probably by 1920. An additional social factor that may have helped further its acceptance was the outlawing of houses of prostitution in 1919. This moved the tango even more firmly into the theatres and the better clubs and dance halls. It is ironic that the tango's association with prostitution has always been one reason given to prove that the tango was criminal in origin. Yet until 1919 prostitution, while strictly regulated, was perfectly legal, no matter what the moral implications.[5] Thus in 1923 the tango could even be danced in the presidential palace in Buenos Aires at a banquet in honor of the Prince of Wales.[6] Thereafter its fate was more a matter of politics than of class, and over the years it suffered numerous suppressions and revivals depending on whether the current government saw it as a source of shame or pride in relation to Argentine identity.

The French had embraced the tango partly by importing the image of the *compadrito;* hence it seems only reasonable that Argentines responded by importing the image of the *Apache.* Writing as Fray Mocho, José Alvirez in May 1912 describes an invitation from a police detective to go and see groups of *Apaches* in Buenos Aires. According to the detective, *Apaches* first appeared in the port city around 1910, and the same bloody, cruel, vengeful life of the *Apache* in Paris was now seen in Buenos Aires. They also had the same kinds of female accomplices, in Buenos Aires called *gigolettes,* who, like the *minas,* were obsessively attached to their men no matter how badly they were treated.

In the same issue, Julio Castellanos describes another Paris custom imported by the people of Buenos Aires: the cabaret. The emphasis in these places was on entertainment for everyone:

> In imitation of the Paris cabarets, they had tried to give the same quaint atmosphere of Montmartre—gracious and picturesque, with the Parisienne good humor, with the same kind of characters, caricatures, and masters of comedy.
>
> Music [plays] . . . Pierrot mimes a ballad to the moon, as a couple tangos in the Paris style.

Castellanos goes on to say that these places were filled with people in Paris fashions dancing the tango in Parisian style—and that many *porteños* considered it particularly bad dancing.[7]

Several other artistic and social elements also affected the changing profile of the tango. Beginning soon after the turn of the twentieth century, women composers and singers of tangos began to be recognized on at least a national level. By the 1920s Rosita Quiroga, Azucena Maizani, Libertad Lamarque, Sofia

Bozan, and others were as popular as their male counterparts. Besides having access to the dance, women of all social classes could now participate in all aspects of both the creation and the consumption of the tango, even though the themes of tango lyrics still focused on male issues. Rosita Quiroga composed the music for the following tango lyric by Eduardo Mendez, a text that sums up the thoughts of one looking back over a lifetime's involvement with the tango:

"Campaneando la vejez" (Considering Old Age), ca. 1920

La luces de la milonga
jamas mis ojos cerraron
y el tango, el bendito tango,
a quien cante con amor
en vez de ser mi desdicha,
como muchas lo culparon,
fue mi palabra de aliento
para luchar con honor.

The lights of the dance hall
never blinded me
and the tango, that blessed tango,
to whom I sang with love
instead of being my misfortune,
as many have blamed him,
was my word of encouragement
to struggle with honor.[8]

Various electronic media also expanded the world of the tango, as radio and film not only brought it to wider audiences but greatly enhanced the opportunities for those hoping for success as tango performers. Not surprisingly, the first Argentine sound film, produced in 1933, was titled *Tango.*[9]

Some of the changes to the tango itself are particularly interesting. By the 1920s the favorite themes and images of betrayal, bitterness, loneliness, and loss were not only well in place but could also be recalled nostalgically over a period of some forty years. This is reflected in a tango poem written in 1927 by Carlos de la Pua, "El entrerriano" (The Man from Entre Rios), published in his 1928 collection of Lunfardo poetry, *La crencha engrasada* (Greasy Hair). It is based on a tango of the same name written in 1897 by Rosendo Mendizabal:

> Entrerriano, Entrerriano, en tu reo canyengue
> va cumpliendo un plenario la emoción del suburbio.
> Me batis suavecito la parola del yungue,
> me ortivás de la faca, de la cana, del lengue,
> del jotraba chorede y del laburo turbio.
>
> Vivirás mientras siga copando la patriada
> un táura arrabalero que despreció la yuta,
> mientras se haga un escruche sin que salga mancada
> mientras taya la grela de la crencha aceitada,
> mientras viva un poeta, un ladron y una puta.
>
> Man from Entre Rios, man from Entre Rios,
> through your complicated tango steps born out of the slums
> you are meeting your responsibility
> of carrying out the spirit of the city's outskirts.
> You told me in your softly spoken words,
> you gave yourself away by your knife,
> your jail time, and by your *compadrito*'s ascot,
> by your honest work and by your crimes.
>
> You will live on in the deeds of others,
> as long as a slum tough makes light of the cops,
> as long as a thief can break and enter without a clue,
> as long as the skirt with the oily hair does her thing,
> as long as there is a poet, a thief, and a whore.[10]

This fatalistic view was also pervasive in tango theatre. Expanding on the role of the tango in the *sainete,* Armando Discepolo created the *grotesco criollo,* or creole tragicomedy. The name came from the sixteenth-century Italian tradition of the *grottesco,* "the art of arriving at the comic via the tragic." Tango lyrics, especially those of Armando's younger brother Enrique, began to reflect *la cachada,* which Donald Castro defines as "the cruel art of making fun of others via self-aggrandizement at the comedic expense of others."[11]

By the 1930s, after the period under consideration here, images of the tango were firmly in place. Rather than reflecting the everyday experiences of the people living in the world of the tango, these images were now conveyed through the *tango-canción* (tango song), created largely by Pablo Contursi[12] and performed by singers such as Carlos Gardel. In addition to the *compadrito,* the male ideal for the *tanguero* embodied a combination of *machismo* and the worldliness of the idle rich, symbolized by the smoking jackets worn by tango singers. Since the tango had been accepted by all classes of society and was no longer exotic, Lunfardo was relegated to the function of adding accents of local color.

The acceptance of the tango abroad and subsequently in all of Argentina had both positive and negative effects. Preservation, pride, identity, and longevity were gained when empowered people adopted the tango. However, some of its colorful character, its uncompromising edginess, and its fearless attitude were lost or smoothed over, becoming a matter of pretense and memory rather than reality. Despite its trials over the last forty to fifty years, the Argentine tango is undergoing an energetic revival today. Both tango dancing and tango music are alive and well, and those who enter the world of the tango today cannot help but experience something of its mysterious past.

4 Tango Music

The guitar still hangs in the clothes closet.
No one sings anything with it nor sounds its strings.
And the lamp in the room also feels your absence
because its glow has no desire to light my sad night.

—from "Mi noche triste" (Buenos Aires)

Tango ankles and Tango knees,
Tango luncheons and Tango teas,
Tango slippers and Tango socks,
Tango petticoats, Tango frocks,
Tango bruises on Tango heads,
Tango blankets and Tango beds,
Tango microbes and Tango quacks,
Tango ointments for Tango backs . . .

—from "Tango Tangle" (London)

Musical Influences on the Early Argentine Tango

 Although this chapter addresses the tango music associated with the habanera rhythm and the dance form from Argentina, neither the word *tango* nor music based on the habanera pattern originated with this type. In 1932, writing in the Argentine newspaper *La prensa,* musicologist Carlos Vega distinguished between the Andalusian tango and the Argentine tango, describing the former in this way:

In the middle of the last century, a species of popular song called tango arose in Andalucia, reaching enormous diffusion and popularity. The text consisted of various quatrains of eight syllables, or an alternation of these with quatrains of five syllables. The guitar accompanied the singers by means of an invariable [pattern], and after the refrain a short instrumental interlude called the *falseta* was heard. The *tango andaluz* was also danced: at first as a woman's solo, later for one or more couples. Man and woman, face to face, marked the rhythm with their feet, doing half-turns and using castanets with their fingers.[1]

According to Vega, Spanish scholars at the end of the nineteenth century determined that the Andalusian tango enjoyed its greatest popularity between 1855 and 1875 and died out as a popular song around 1880. It continued to appear after 1880 as one of the popular carnival songs performed onstage, and despite the increasing decadence of its lyrics its musical quality was high enough to inspire its inclusion in the more artistic *zarzuelas*. The lyrics of the Andalusian tango followed a customary pattern of allusion to entertaining or notable aspects of everyday life. The name of each tango was derived from one of the characters in its text—for example, the tango "of the housekeeper" or "of the cowboy."

Vega believed that somewhere there was an original text of several stanzas and a single refrain, and that sometimes new stanzas fitting a new anecdote were added on, whether or not they related to the original. He cited the following examples:

The tango "of the *casera* [housekeeper]" owes its name to a popular protagonist character. . . . The *señora casera* participates in various dialogues, more or less related to her duties, that create a group of variations in which are found many of the most interesting examples of the genre. By chance, it was included in the *zarzuelas*.

The tango "of the *sombreritos*" owes its appearance to the imposition in Seville, in the year 1880, of a certain style of Austrian hat, enormous and overloaded with adornments, and frankly ridiculous in the eyes of the people.

The tango "of the *vaquita*" was sung with stanzas that protested the quality of beef distributed at that time by Sevillian butchers.[2]

The similarity to the witty, humorous, or satiric type of lyrics from Argentina discussed in chapter 1 is clear. What is different about the Andalusian tango is that often the same music served for many different texts, or combinations of texts, with whatever minor musical variations were needed to accommodate the number of syllables in a line.

Vega goes on to say that his Spanish scholars were unable to supply examples of Andalusian tango music, despite their success at collecting lyrics, and he felt that the surviving classical versions in the *zarzuelas* were too much changed to be reliable guides. However, Vega engaged in some rather clever fieldwork, speculating that there might be Andalusians living in Buenos Aires who, in the 1930s, might still recall the old melodies of the 1880s. He claims considerable success, with many independent contacts yielding surprisingly consistent results, and his article includes part of the music for the tango "of the *casera.*"

Vega thought that the most significant connection between the Andalusian and Argentine tangos lay in the rhythmic base common to both: the habanera. He again cites as evidence the early Spanish collectors of Andalusian texts, who, although they gave no specific examples, describe the music accompanying them as a "species of tango habanera." Additional evidence came from Juan Alvarez, author of *Origines de la musica Argentina* (Origins of Argentine Music) (c. 1900), who, like Vega, believed that he had found "notable similarity between the [Argentine] tango, the habanera, and the *milonga*" and concluded that they were "different aspects of the same thing." Alvarez had defended an

African origin for all three types, yet he said that "in a collection of Andalusian pieces edited in Spain and with the heading 'tango' [he] found the typical accompaniment of our *milongas*."[3]

No one in 1930s Argentina would have been surprised to hear that Spanish *zarzuelas* containing tango songs had been performed in Buenos Aires in the 1880s and 1890s. Vega carried the point further, however, and asserted that the very early, unpublished Andalusian tangos were also widely circulated independently of the theatres in Buenos Aires as early as the 1870s. These songs began to be Argentine when local wits adapted tales and episodes of life in the port city to the Spanish melodies. Vega describes his discoveries:

> More interesting . . . to us is the assertion that those Andalusian tangos, popular and unpublished, those first ones of the 1870s and 1880s, were cultivated in Argentina with the same intent as in Andalucia, identical music and verses alluding to local events, sung in the streets.
>
> An article published in *La prensa* on October 17, 1926, gave me a profitable reference. It was titled "Buenos Aires around the year 1888" and was signed don Rodolfo Senet.
>
> The author remembers the omnibuses pulled by horses that appeared in the year 1888. "The coaches were comfortable," said Sr. Senet, "and the service good, but even [the routine service] did not rapidly gain public approval; on the contrary, *milongas* foretold the next breakdown." The characteristic *si, si, si* of the refrain convinced me immediately that we are not dealing with a *milonga*, but rather with a *tango andaluz*. The music would decide it. But, how to obtain the music? Persuaded of the shadowy link that lyrics and music maintain in our memory—well demonstrated here—I visited Sr. Senet and acquired the musical version presented on this same page with which the reader can amuse himself by an easy comparison: it is a simple question of the music of the *tango andaluz* "of the *casera*" being clearly visible in spite of the variations produced by its adaptation to a new text.[4]

a.

b.

Example 4.1. Examples of tangos compared by Carlos Vega: (*a*) the earlier Andalusian version and (*b*) a later version found in Argentina. Carlos Vega, "El tango andaluz y el tango argentine," *La prensa* (Buenos Aires), April 10, 1932.

Apparently this melody was so popular that many different texts were adapted to it. Vega's quotations of the Andalusian and later Argentine version are included as Example 4.1., parts a and b, respectively.

In the second half of his article, Vega addresses the confusion surrounding the terms *tango, habanera,* and *milonga* as they were used inconsistently for songs, instrumental pieces, and dances. He gives five categories where names were mixed and matched: (1) the habanera called tango, (2) the *tango andaluz* called habanera, (3) the *tango andaluz* called *milonga,* (4) the habanera called *milonga,* and (5) the *milonga* called tango. In the first four cases he cites examples of music that appeared at one time with one label and at one time with another, depending on editor's choices or popular usage. In the fifth example, however, he builds a case for the development of the 1880s song and dance form known as the Argentine tango. Vega says that around 1880 in Buenos Aires, several kinds of popular songs coexisted that used the habanera as a common rhythmic base. One form was the Cuban habanera, which Vega claims appeared around the mid-nineteenth century and had the highest artistic quality and the widest influence. There was also the *tango andaluz,* discussed earlier, which was less widely known at midcentury. The third type of song was the *milonga* from the Argentine pampas—the best-known song type, but at midcentury not yet called *milonga.*

Vega deals with the common appearance of the basic habanera rhythm by saying that this rhythm was common to all Hispanic American music. He places the earliest appearances of this rhythm in the notations of rabbinical collections in late medieval Spain[5] and therefore does not credit the rhythm of the tango to any one modern Hispanic or African source.

Of the three song types Vega describes, the *tango andaluz* and the habanera had choreographies. The *milonga,* according to Vega, did not acquire a connection with dance until around 1870, when it joined the others in Buenos Aires. Vega explains how they all joined together to form the Argentine tango:

> The *milonga* . . . acquired choreographic possibilities through its proximity to the habanera, quickly carried out by the *compadrito* with great originality. In spite of that, the *milonga* has nothing to do with the habanera, either melodically or choreographically, although when the musicians exhausted the repertoire of *milongas* at the dances, habaneras served up the same beat to the same effect. The very interesting figure of the *compadrito* still has not been fully studied. To give the *milonga* its choreography, they had nothing more suitable to use than their own contortions, slips, and slides, which had distinguished their own style of dancing the mazurka, the polka, or the habanera; and when these disappeared,[6] all of the new choreography had to be absorbed by the *milonga* and then by the Argentine tango. The momentum of this intermingling continued from 1880–1900.

Vega concludes by claiming that composers for some time continued to write Cuban habaneras, Andalusian tangos, and *milongas,* as well as the new *porteño* song derived from all three popular forms. He says that the new song did not yet deserve the name "tango." Only when the small supply of Andalusian tango melodies had been overused and composers began to write new melodies for the *porteño* songs did the true Argentine tango appear. In addition, Vega claims that the shift away from the familiar Andalusian melodies precipitated the move toward tragic, darker pieces and away from the light, humorous, satiric parodies of the *tango andaluz,* and that this shift did not take place until after 1900. This left Argentina with two distinctive types (occasionally only distinguishable to Argentines): the more cheerful *milonga* and the darker, more tragic tango.[7]

Another example of a possible Spanish *tango andaluz,* "La Guajirita del Yumuri," dates from before 1888 (the year of composer I. Hernandez's death). The lyrics reflect the style of the *tango andaluz,* although it is simply labeled *tango,* and its music shows the habanera rhythm and sequential melodic line found in many later tangos from Buenos Aires. Excerpts from this tango and a translation of its lyrics are found in Example 4.2.

Example 4.2. Excerpts from (*a*) the introduction, (*b*) the verse, and (*c*) the chorus of "La guajirita del Yumuri." Part *d* is my translation of the text.

d. *La Guajirita del Yumuri*

When a cloud the color of roses
Says to the flowers that come in April
I thirst for love, to see you, Beauty,
On the banks of the Yumuri.

The birds gather, the river murmurs,
All who are there tell me to be calm.
The peasant girl of Yumuri has my heart,
The peasant girl of Yumuri.

The birds sing, the river murmurs,
All who are there tell me,
The birds sing, the river murmurs,
All who are there tell me.

Today there are those who disagree with Vega's interpretation of the *milonga*'s role in the emergence of the tango. Many Argentines consider the two to be, both musically and choreographically, entirely separate types that never commingled, despite their common rhythmic base. And certainly the *milonga* dance is very different from the tango in Argentina. Moreover, most scholars consider as Argentine tangos only pieces written from the 1880s onward, when the texts reflected life in Buenos Aires and the composers were citizens of the port city. Nonetheless, Vega's analysis of the relationship between the Spanish and Argentine musical tangos is one of the clearest and most articulate to date.

Native scholars of tango history tend to speculate about the identity of the first true Argentine tango. Most agree that the strongest contender is a tango titled "Dame la lata," written by Juan Perez. Although there is disagreement as to the date of its composition, with 1870, 1871, 1880, and 1888 given as possibilities, most agree that this tango was well known by the early 1880s. Blas Matamoro, writing about early examples of the genre, provides a footnote that appears to connect the title's meaning with one of the ongoing myths about where and by whom the tango was danced:

Andres Chinarro, in his book *El tango y su rebeldia* (Continental Services, Buenos Aires, 1965), said, regarding the strange name of this tango: "*Lata* was a chip that the madam in a brothel collected from her [employees] for each client and that had a value of fifty percent of the price. The pimp collected on a regular basis, and thus he said, 'Give me the *lata*.'" Lopecito [a popular media figure] preferred to give it a more decent meaning. . . . We heard him say on the radio that the *lata* was the admission ticket to a dance hall.[8]

Contained in the title of one piece of music, then, we have one of the central and most disputed issues of the tango's origins: whether it was only danced in brothels by whores and criminals or whether it was danced at poor but essentially decent dance halls. Certainly both meanings could have been in circulation in Buenos Aires, and for those who made little or no distinction in propriety between a brothel and a dance hall, the difference was of little importance. Perhaps both were true—but the seamier one was deemed more memorable.

Instruments of the Early Tango

Most Argentine historians who began researching the early tango in the 1940s and 1950s recognized two periods of composition between 1875 and 1925, the *Guarda Vieja* (Old Guard) and the *Guarda Nueva* (New Guard). There is, as with most aspects of tango history, debate about when and why the Old Guard gave way to the New Guard. Some scholars put the year at 1915, arguing that a large increase in recordings occurred then, with larger professional orchestras producing music for wide public consumption on phonograph and radio. Others say that 1924 should mark the change, because that year saw the last public appearances of the Old Guard composers.[9]

The instruments on which these early tangos of the Old Guard were performed were the typical ones of dance hall pickup bands: guitar, violin, flute, and, slightly later, the piano and the bando-

Figure 4.1. An *organito de la tarde* from around 1900, for sale in the San Telmo market of Buenos Aires. Author's photograph.

neon (or bandonion), an accordion-like instrument imported from Germany. This configuration of instruments became known as the *orquesta tipica* and, although increased in size by the doubling of instruments and the occasional addition of the contrabass, remained a viable ensemble. The guitar had always been a favorite instrument of the countryside, particularly for the *gauchos, payadores* (wandering poet-musicians), and other wanderers who left the pampas and fed the new mixture of cultures in Buenos Aires. Flutists, pianists, and violinists always seemed to be around when dance bands were forming. Many of the musicians who played tangos became widely known for that specialty and are now as well known by name as any of the famous composers to the true devotees of tango music in Argentina.

One unique solo instrument for the tango was the *organito de la tarde.* This was a small keyboard instrument rather like a personal-size calliope. It was in a box, with the mouths of the pipes pointing forward, and the player stood behind at the keyboard. Often there were two wheels on the front corners of the box to assist in moving the instrument about. A self-contained bellows supplied the wind for the pipes. The *organito de la tarde* was an instrument for street musicians and was most likely played alone. Its sound is strident, often out of tune, and has the familiar chiff and breathy sound of most larger calliopes.

The other unique instrument was the bandoneon. Heinrich Band (1821–60), a German merchant, publisher, and instrument manufacturer, is credited with its invention, although he did not claim this distinction. His family had a long tradition of selling musical instruments, and Heinrich, like his father, played in a local band. The bandoneon was probably invented sometime around 1846 and was available for purchase by 1850. Band placed the following advertisement in a local newspaper, the *Crefelder Zeitung,* on December 10, 1850: "To friends of the accordion. By way of a new invention, we have once again remarkably perfected our accordions, and these new instruments, round or octagonal, from 88 to 144 voices, are available at our store."[10] In this case, each vibrating steel reed counts as a voice. The term *bandonion* did not appear until 1856, when music dealer Johann Schmitz advertised the instrument in the *Crefelder Jahrbuch:* "Accordions, Concertinas (also known as Bandonions) of 20 to 22 tones, with changes of octaves, which surpass all the portable wind instruments made up until now."[11] Despite its common usage, the word *bandoneon* was never registered as a trademark name for a new instrument, and no patent was ever issued for its creation.

It turns out that the actual inventor of the bandoneon was C. Zimmerman, who exhibited it at the Paris Exposition of 1849. Zimmerman's "Carlsfeld Concertina" made its way to Crefeld and was the instrument that Band perfected and sold. Zimmerman sold his factory to Ernst Louis Arnold, and the instrument developed by this firm found passage to Argentina with German immigrants. Ironically, the instrument that gave voice to the *mufarse* of the *porteño* slums was known only to the upper class in Germany, due to the expense of both the instrument and the music to play on it. Only toward the end of the nineteenth century did German middle- and working-class musicians have access to the bando-neon. An Arnold son, Alfred, went into competition with the family firm, and his instrument became the bandoneon of choice for professional tango musicians after the turn of the century. The preferred model was inlaid with mother-of-pearl and had 142 voices, and each steel reed was filed by hand.[12]

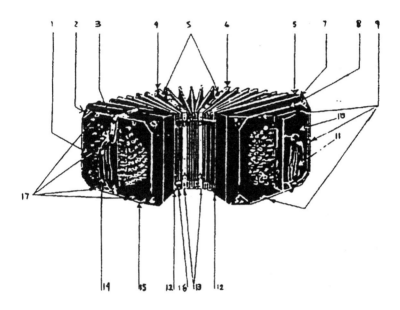

1. Caja de resonancia derecha. 2. Ochava con la lira. 3. Palanca de aire. 4. Chapas de adorno. 5. Ganchos. 6. Marcos tapa. 7. Caja de resonancia izquierda. 8. Media caña. 9. Tres tornillos. 10. Tapa acústica. 11. Manija madera de los bajos. 12. Esquineros laterales. 13. Marcos centrales. 14. Esquineros chicos. 15. Media caña. 16. Manija manera de los cantos. 17. Cuatro tornillos palomita.

Figure 4.2. Schematic description of a bandoneon, from Oscar D. Zucchi, "El bando-neon en el tango," in *La historia del tango,* vol. 5 (Buenos Aires: Ediciones Corregi-dor, 1977), 658. The captions translate as follows: 1. Right resonating chamber. 2. Transposing device. 3. Air lever. 4. Decorative veneer. 5. Hooks. 6. Top frame-work. 7. Left resonating chamber. 8. Middle reed. 9. Three screws. 10. Acoustical plate. 11. Wooden handle for the bass. 12. Side corner pieces. 13. Center frame-work. 14. Small corner-pieces. 15. Middle reed. 16. Handle for the treble. 17. Four "palomita" screws.

The bandoneon had a profound effect on the development of tango music. Arturo Penon, whose thoughts on the social milieu of the early tango were presented in chapter 1, had the privilege of knowing and making music with some of the great *bandoneon-istas*. He described how the bandoneon was welcomed by the *porteño* musicians and, in typical Buenos Aires fashion, promptly acquired several nicknames, including "bellows," "worm," and "cage."[13] In addition to its usefulness as a pickup instrument for entertainment at local parties and weddings, the bandoneon affected tango music itself. Pennon believed that the tango

> was never the same after becoming intertwined with the ban[d]onion. This is because of the difficulties the instrument presented to anyone who tried to get the hang of it. Before the arrival of the bandonion in Buenos Aires, the tango employed a $\frac{2}{4}$ beat, quick moving, and *allegre con moto.* The instruments usually performed in its execution—flute, clarinet, guitar—allowed the musicians to play at great speeds. But because of the new fingering problems posed by the bandonion, and of the absence of established methods of execution and, sometimes, because of the inability of the musicians to read music, the new instrument changed the tango, making it slower.

Penon then compares the limitations of the early bandoneonists to those of guitar-playing *gauchos,* who used a simple, play-by-ear system of three basic chords:

> The situation of the primitive bandonionist was not dissimilar: he had to consult other musicians on questions of proper technique or . . . to recreate by ear the sounds coming from a phonograph. Thus, with the arrival of the bandonion, the tango split into several styles, each defined by its own tempo, without modifying the scores themselves. Later, composers replaced the $\frac{2}{4}$ beat with a $\frac{4}{8}$ beat. Here no doubt is the reason that people who heard the primitive tango recall that the bandonion made it a sad music. This adjective is perhaps not the most adequate, but the people who make this assertion are less mis-

taken than those who trace the "sadness" of the tango directly
to Gardel. Before Gardel became a tango singer, the tango had
already been modified by the bandonion: the formerly mischie-
vous, lively dance had become cadenced, slow, intimate, med-
itative—epithets that seem more apt to me than "sad."[14]

Penon's account attributes the tango's change of identity to
one of darkness and sadness to a different cause than that cited by
Carlos Vega, and it also places the change about fifteen to twenty
years earlier. Since the theories of change each writer supports address such different aspects of tango creation, it seems unwise to
choose between them, particularly since the sociological changes
occurring in Buenos Aires in the 1880s and soon thereafter were
creating a class of melancholy displaced people who voiced their
discontent in the tango. It seems more reasonable that a unique
convergence of influences—some ongoing, like the sound of the
bandoneon; some short-term, like the *tango andaluz*—came together at a fortuitous moment to create a new music for a people
in need of a musical identity.

It is interesting that so many of the great moments in the
early history of the tango began through an influence from outside
Argentina. If a Spanish song and a German instrument in the earliest years brought it to the lower class, the enthusiasm with
which the French embraced the tango eventually led all of Argentine society to claim it as their own. Penon describes the path of
transmission:

> Before they welcomed this music, the French were familiar
> with Argentina primarily through a substantial trade in meat and
> grain raised in our countryside. It was after the establishment of
> this commerce that a few tango musicians started to travel to
> the French capital, such as Alfredo Gobbi Sr., Flora Rodriguez,
> and Angel Villoldo who . . . were sent to Paris by the firm Gath
> and Chaves[15] to make recordings. These musicians were pre-
> ceded by other Argentine travelers . . . who . . . went to obnu-
> bilate[16] themselves in the City of Light. Armed with their valu-

able pesos, they adventured into the mythology of champagne, pretty women, and dissolute lifestyles that this capital ceaselessly promoted.

The guardians of this mythology coddled their new guests. . . . Thus they began to hire performers who sang Argentine songs, acted out humorous sketches and played primitive tangos by the composers of the day, such as Gobbi, Villoldo, and Domingo Campoamor. And these visitors came to enjoy that which, at home, was anathema.[17] . . . Upon returning to Argentina, these travelers conveyed to their friends their sudden passion for a music that had hitherto been considered plebeian.

By 1916, various popular and workers' factions had achieved political power, and there was universal suffrage in Argentina. Penon believes that the permeation and visibility of the working class made their culture fashionable and acceptable, and the tango was one of the major beneficiaries of this new thinking.

This led to an unprecedented surge in the popularity of the tango in the working class suburbs and its introduction to the centre of the city. At the same time, the centre ceased to be the exclusive domain of a minority. At this time, a rapid professionalisation of tango musicians took place: this was the period when some of those who had come from afar, like Firpo, Arolas, Francisco Canaro, and the violinist Tito Roccatagliata, were able to abandon their trades as blacksmiths, housepainters, carters and bricklayers to devote themselves exclusively to music.

It's easy to imagine how this process enriched the tango. Bandonionists, for example, were now able to acquaint themselves with many works—not only those of popular origin. They began to study notation, leaving behind aural techniques in favour of learning harmony, composition, and systems and techniques which allowed new explorations of the instrument itself. Other musicians, particularly pianists, helped introduce them to musical structure and notation. Also, the tango was en-

riched by the emergence of new poets, and conservatory—
trained musicians, many of them children of immigrants or immigrants themselves.[18]

Musicians and Composers of Early Tangos

As Penon points out, the musicians who played and developed the
tango in its early years had a variety of musical backgrounds and careers. Many were self-taught, learning both their instruments and
the music they played by watching and listening to other musicians. Often they could not read music. Others had some formal
training, could read music, and had the skills to develop their own
compositional traits and styles. Some worked full-time as musicians, performing and teaching, while others earned most of their
livelihood at mundane careers and joined the nightlife in the city as
members of various dance and tango bands. Yet when one studies
their backgrounds, a pattern emerges that places them right in the
middle of the social structure that produced the tango. These main
players were not classically trained composers imitating popular
music. A brief look at the careers of several prominent composers
illustrates the pattern of their early lives.

Angel Villoldo (1864–1919) had a variety of jobs in his early
years, including typesetter, reporter, actor, and singer. By 1890 he
was playing tangos on guitar and harmonica in the dance halls
and cafés, and he also studied piano and violin. His tangos, for
which he often wrote both words and music, were immediately
popular. Among those still heard today are "El Choclo" and "Ele-
gancias." Villoldo was one of the composer/players invited to
travel to France around 1907 to perform their music in the clubs
and to record tangos for Gath and Chaves. In later years he also
wrote and composed for the theatre and created sketches of
porteño life for *Fray Mocho* and *Caras y caretas,* two of the popular Argentine magazines of the day.

Rosendo Mendizabal (1868–1913) came from a poor family that nonetheless saw to it that he received a good education. He began his career by teaching music skills and piano to the children of Buenos Aires aristocrats. He also began to play piano in the dance halls of his own neighborhood, and earned a reputation as a premier interpreter of *milongas.* By 1897 both his compositions—which include "Z Club," "Reina de Saba," and "Laura"— and his playing in dance bands had attracted a loyal following. Mendizabal was respected as one of the most gracious of the tango composers, although his work fell into obscurity after his death. He was rediscovered in the first tango revival of the 1930s and has remained popular ever since.

Enrique Saborido (1877–1941), one of the few tango greats born outside Argentina, came from a working-class family in Montevideo, an important Uruguayan tango city across the river Plata from Buenos Aires. There the *milonga* was already very popular, and the tango was just beginning to take hold. The Saboridos also insisted that their sons be well educated, and Enrique completed formal studies before taking up the violin. His debut as a tango player occurred in 1904, and one of his best-known works is "La morocha," with words by Villoldo. Saborido started his own dance hall in 1912, and he traveled to the clubs of Paris. "La Morocha" became a favorite dance piece for all levels of Parisian society, and Saborido was called the "King of Tango" in the Paris newspapers. His fame in Paris helped, in turn, to legitimize the *danza-canción* form of the tango in the minds of Argentine society.

Juan Maglio (Pacho) (1880–1934) was learning to play the bandoneon by ear by age twelve, although his father insisted that he also train as a mechanic. A neighborhood teacher and bandoneon player noticed Juan's potential and offered free lessons. By 1899 the boy had formed his own small tango orchestra, which quickly became well known and well regarded in the big Buenos Aires clubs. Soon he combined forces with his brother Francisco.

His first tango was "El zurdo." Maglio recorded for Columbia and toured both Argentina and Uruguay.

Roberto Firpo (b. 1884) was a pianist and a student of the noted music teacher Alfredo Bevilacqua. He played in a variety of tango and regular orchestras and, with Canaro, Arolas, and others, formed his own tango orchestra in 1917. His first tangos included "La chola," "El companche," and "La guacha Manuela," all composed in 1907. Firpo faithfully adhered to the old style and remained true to earlier rules of interpretation even into the era of the New Guard—a practice that earned him many loyal fans.

Juan de Dios Filiberto (1885–1964) also came from a poor background and joined various groups of anarchists in his youth. His father ran a *casa de diversiones* where Villoldo and many other early tango greats spent time. Filiberto was a famous exponent of the *tango-canción,* and Carlos Gardel recorded many of his songs. He composed his first *tango-canción,* "Guaymallen," in 1915.

Vicente Greco (Garrote) (1888–1924) had a natural musical talent apparent from early childhood. His parents encouraged the development of his talent in school, and he was soon singing in carnivals and theatres. Later he learned to play the flute; when he was fourteen years old, his family and neighbors took up a collection and bought him a bandoneon. He began to play in the local tango bands, and by 1910 he was composing his own tangos, including "La infanta" and "El Pibe."

Francisco Canaro (1888–1964) had a varied career as a violinist, composer, orchestra director, and theatre musician. He had a prolific recording career, working for both Columbia and Disco National Odeon. In 1925 he made the journey to Paris, and from then on his career expanded to include film music. His first tango was "La barra fuerte," composed in 1908. Canaro was one of very few tango greats to enjoy lasting financial success.

Eduardo Arolas (1892–1924) was an outstanding bandoneonist and an inspired composer who helped build the bridge between the Old and New Guards. His innovations include passages in which the melody is paralleled in thirds or octaves and experimentation with use of the cello in the *orquesta típica.* He composed his first tango, "Una noche de Garufa," in 1909. Arolas learned music theory and notation fairly late in life, although he had a notable career in various tango orchestras in Paris and Argentina and recorded for Victor. Although he was known to have tuberculosis, his sudden death in Paris was unexpected.

Despite individual differences, several common threads link the lives of these men. Almost all were born in poor neighborhoods, displayed an early talent for music, and were helped along by family, neighbors, and local tango musicians. All made the rounds of the local orchestras and clubs; many went to Paris display their talent and their compositions; many recorded for major companies; and many formed their own orchestras. On a sadder note, many also died fairly young, and most died in poverty and obscurity. That they are remembered fondly today by tango scholars and fans is a tribute to the endurance of their music and of the tango itself.[19]

Tango Music

Tango music shares several characteristics with most other types of Western social dance music. Almost without exception, phrases are eight bars in length, and an even number of phrases makes up a section. There are commonly two or three sections, perhaps four if the material of the first section is written out again between the second and third sections. The third section may be labeled a trio. All the sections, including the trio, are generally enclosed by repeat signs. Tango songs often have a repeating chorus between stanzas and a *dal segno* to a final chorus at the end.

Tonalities move between closely related keys. The dominant and subdominant are the most common secondary keys for tangos in major keys, and the major dominant and relative major are predominant for tangos in minor keys. Modulations within sections are uncommon beyond the occasional brief secondary dominant, and the shift to a new key for a new section is generally abrupt, without much in the way of transitional harmonies. A great deal of tango music was published in piano arrangements for the general public. Most often the keys chosen were those with few accidentals, but arrangements exist in keys as difficult as D♭. Orchestral arrangements of tangos generally ventured slightly further afield, but even these tended not to move beyond E♭ as a primary key. The harmonies within sections are generally built on the diatonic scale. Even when a melody is somewhat chromatic, the underlying chords stay within the key, using simple progressions that are easy to pick up by ear. Cadences are generally authentic or half cadences, again making the tonality easy to follow without notation.

Within these seeming limitations, composers created a diverse and varied repertoire. One of the elements that allowed variation was the habanera rhythm pattern. In piano arrangements the habanera often comprised the sole rhythm of the left-hand part. This part could consist largely of a single line that outlined the harmony in the familiar rhythm pattern, as in Joaquin Cassado's "Flor de Canela," shown in Example 4.3.

Example 4.3. Joaquin Cassado, "Flor de Canela" (Paris: Durand et Cie., 1913).

Block chords could lend a percussive effect to any variation of the habanera pattern, as shown in the second section of Juan de Dios Filiberto's "Langosta" in Example 4.4.

Example 4.4. Juan de Dios Filiberto, "Langosta," words by Juan A.
Bruno (Buenos Aires: Pirovano, n.d.).

Early tangos tended to use some form of habanera consis-
tently throughout a piece, but gradually composers began to ex-
periment with other materials for the left hand. Variations could
include interpolating other rhythms between appearances of the
habanera pattern or choosing a variation in the rhythm of the habanera itself. Examples of these treatments of the left hand appear
in Example 4.5.

Gradually the variation ♫♩♫ began to predominate, and
after about 1920 a marchlike rhythm of even quarter or eighth
notes formed the typical pattern for the lowest parts, as shown in

Example 4.5. A variety of possible treatments of the left-hand or bass parts of
early tangos.

the left-hand part of Example 4.6, C. A. Bixio's "Il tango della pampa."

In European orchestral arrangements the habanera is almost always shared by several instruments. A sample distribution can be seen in Example 4.7, "El irresistible." In such arrangements the

Example 4.6. C. A. Bixio, "Il tango della pampa" ([Rome]: n.p., n.d.).

piano is often used for a percussive, chordal effect as well as doubling some of the melodic material.

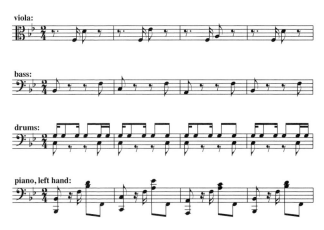

Example 4.7. Parts comprising the habanera of L. Logatti's "El irresistible" (New York: Schirmer, 1913).

The habanera rhythm did not remain confined to the left hand or lower orchestral parts. As tango composition became more sophisticated, composers began to use the habanera throughout the

Example 4.8. E. Arolas, "Place Pigalle" (Buenos Aires: Ricordi, n.d.).

texture. Melodies in habanera rhythm were not uncommon, as in the first section of "Place Pigalle," shown in Example 4.8.

When a composer chose to insert a melodic passage in the bass line, the upper lines would carry the rhythm. By the end of the period under study here, tangos might refer to the habanera rhythm only at the ends of phrases or sections to establish the piece's identity as a tango. "Langosta" (Example 4.4) is such a tango, with the habanera appearing only at the end of each section.

Composers also used a variety of ideas in tango melodies. The majority of melodies are singable, as the tango is never far from its roots in song. Many tangos originally had words, even though the words might not be used in performance today. Both sustained and rhythmically active melodies are found in the repertoire, and there might be a section in each style; alternatively, the stanzas might be in one style with the chorus in the other. Compositional devices include sequences of either a brief motive or a longer line, as in the first section of "Il tango della pampa" (Example 4.6). Related to the sequence, but with a character unique to the tango, is the appearance of sixteenth notes within a very small range, creating a constantly busy sound. José Padula's "9 de Julio" shows this kind of countermelody to a vocal line (Example 4.9), and it is not unreasonable to see in such examples the beginnings of the modern style of bandoneon or violin accompaniment used by Astor Piazzolla and others.

All of these patterns may be combined with chromatic lines

Example 4.9. José Paula, "9 de Julio" (Buenos Aires: Perrotti, 1918). The left-hand piano part consists of chords in a habanera pattern.

or, less often, arpeggios. Another option chosen by tango composers is to repeat two phrases of melody in alternation, varying the end of the last phrase slightly to accommodate concerns of text or cadence. "Langosta," shown again in Example 4.10, is such a piece. Melodic phrases in tangos use both the concave and convex arch shapes as well as the shape that circles within a small range, as shown in Example 4.9.

Example 4.10. Two parallel melodic phrases from Filiberto's "Langosta."

One distinctive and curious aspect of tango composition is the continued presence of triple-meter or waltz sections long after the habanera and its variations firmly established duple meter for the tango. Chapter 5 discusses the mention of the waltz in the earliest known tango description and matches the description to a possible music type. The description and the music that fits it date from the 1850s, some thirty years before the date acknowledged as the beginning of the Buenos Aires tango. Yet triple meter continues to appear in the tango music of Argentina, Europe, and the United States throughout the ragtime era.

Tango composers developed several ways of using triplets or triple meter. One of the most common, and the one that is tied most closely to the idea of including the waltz within the tango, was to take the two beats per measure of $\frac{2}{4}$ time and, without changing their tempo, turn them into two beats of compound or $\frac{6}{8}$ meter. Each half of a measure would then be equal to one bar of waltz, played in a comfortable tempo that could accommodate both dances (see chapter 5 for a further discussion of the mechanics involved). Example 4.11, Antonio Olague's "Cloe," is an early (1885) example of music that uses the habanera for the first section and the waltz for the second.

Example 4.11. Antonio Olague, "Cloe" (N.p.: n.p., 1885). Part *a* is from the habanera or tango section; *b* is from the waltz section.

In another example, "Las luces de los angeles," by Ortiz and Tejada, only about 25 percent of its music is in habanera while the rest is in waltz, yet the piece is labeled a tango.

A more subtle use of triplets was obtained by placing the melody in triplets against a strong habanera in the accompaniment. Example 4.12, Logatti's "El irresistible," illustrates this method of placing triplets against habanera patterns.

Perhaps the most subtle use was that of placing fast triplets into a duple melody as ornaments or accents. Many of these triplets sound like the kinds of turns or mordents musicians might

Example 4.12. The triplet melody from Logatti's "El irresistible" against a conflation of the parts involved in creating the habanera.

use instinctively to ornament a melody; others seem integrated into the melodic material as necessary elements of the tune. Example 4.3, "Flor de Canela," has elements of the first type; Example 4.12, "El irresistible," has elements of the second. Possibly the combination of habanera and waltz was not exclusive to the early tango, as pieces from Mexico and the United States or Europe combine the two rhythms. Some are labeled "tango," while others have a more generic title, such as Charles Puerner's "Hispania—Fantasie."

One unique aspect of European and North American ragtime dance music was applied to the tango. Many pieces of ragtime dance music bear labels denoting more than one type of dance. Dancers were encouraged to adapt their personal repertoire of steps to fit multiple tempi and rhythms, and composers wanted their music to be just as versatile. Pieces might be intended for one-step, two-step, or foxtrot, inclusively. The tango was soon added to the mix, creating titles such as James White's "Just Enough Spice, Tango—One Step—Turkey Trot" or F. H. Losey's "Chow Chow, One or Two Step or Tango." This music combines the rhythms and harmonies of the tango with the more upbeat, lighthearted feel of European dance music. Labels combining tango with polka or maxixe constitute a special category. The maxixe was a Brazilian two-step (a smooth, turning polka without a hop). Since people tended to lump all South American music together, and since the habanera rhythm also appears in the maxixe, European and U.S. composers offered selections labeled as suitable for either dance. Example 4.13, V. Grau's "Maurice Polka

Tango (La coquette)," shows the combination of the traditional maxixe rhythm ♫♫♫ with the usual maxixe version of the habanera ♩. ♪ ♪ in which the third note rather than the fourth is the lowest pitch.

Example 4.13. V. Grau, "Maurice Polka Tango (La coquette)" (London: Jos. W. Stern & Co., 1914).

European and North American composers continued the tradition of writing words for their tangos, although they did so less often than the Argentines and without the introspective, tragic manner found in so many tangos from Buenos Aires. Where Argentine composers looked inward, writing of the individual's grief and travail or at least of incidents in personal, everyday life, composers from Europe and the United States looked outward, placing the tango alongside the cheerful one-steps, foxtrots, and novelty songs that sang of life as a big party or gala ball where everyone is witty, clever, and beautiful. Such an example is found in "La momme tango," billed as "The Fox-Trot—Tango Dance Hit of Paris," with lyrics by Dorothy Terriss and music by Emile Doloire of the Folies Bergères:

> It's the Kid, it's the Kid
> It's the "peppy" little Tango Kid,
> So petite, oh so sweet,
> Some fast "steppy" little Tango Kid.
> There she goes, on her toes,
> Watch her now as she kicks off the lid,
> Give her half a chance,
> Into your heart she'll dance,
> That happy snappy Tango Kid!

Another typical example is "The Tango in the Sky," with words and music by Halsey K. Mohr:

Verse:
One day the Sun announced a dance,
in the ballroom of the sky.
He told them all the merry news,
As he went rolling by,
Then he called on Jupiter Pluvius,
For his orchestra to play,
And the price of admission to this wonderful dance,
Was a tiny silv'ry ray,
From East and West came all the rest,
At the closing of the day:
Chorus:
When the great big Dip, Dip, Dip, Dip, Dipper
Did the Tango in the sky,
All the stars were led by Mars,
As the clouds went rolling by,
When Jupiter swayed with Venus,
How the Great Big Bear did play,
When the great big Dipper did the Tango,
On the great big Milky Way.
Verse:
When all the stars had danced around,
And the band had played a tune,
Old Mars announced the presence
Of his old pal "Mister Moon,"
In the Moon's bright spotlight,
Satellites floated gently through the air,
And they all started laughing at the wonderful tricks,
Performed by Mister Bear,
And then the Sun sent early dawn,
And they scattered everywhere.
Repeat Chorus

Although many of the tangos from Europe and the United States shared these characteristics, or were at least a bit on the charming and sentimental side, both the tragic and the cheerful types of Argentine tango music were highly prized there as well. Many of the tango musicians and composers who went to Paris published their music in Paris, London, Berlin, New York, and other cities. Thus many of the tangos most people today recognize—for example, "Adios muchachos" or "El choclo"—have been famous internationally since their composition.

The music of the Buenos Aires tango, despite the myths that question the morality of its origins, has become universal. In the *porteño* city today it remains a cherished and unifying icon for a country with a diverse heritage. Astor Piazzolla and others have brought to it the most up-to-date aspects of musical style and performance practice in the current revival of tango composition. Yet the old favorites live on, showing themselves highly adaptable to listeners, singers, and dancers of the modern Argentine, modern ballroom, and historic styles of tango dancing.

5 Tangos in Waltz Time

They turn in the Valse, at their pleasure.

—Charles Durang, *The Fashionable Dancer's Casket* (1856)

 The tango that developed in France and the United States in the early twentieth century is familiar to many people as a rather slow couple dance, with distinctive music based on duple-meter habanera rhythm. Less familiar, perhaps, are the tango's early roots in an Argentine dance of the 1880s, and its more distant ancestry in the *milonga,* the Spanish tango, and various Cuban and African dances. Several types of duple-meter music were called "tangos" in Argentina, including marches, habaneras, and tango songs. Evidence exists, however, to suggest that triple or compound meters were also significant for both music and dance in the mid-nineteenth-century tango.

The earliest evidence connecting the tango and triple meter appears in an unlikely source: *The Fashionable Dancer's Casket,* a Philadelphia dance manual of 1856. That a description of a tango appears this early in a source from the United States is surprising enough, but even more intriguing are its link to a Paris dance master and its musical implications. The manual is a collection of instructions for the popular ballroom dances of the day, written by Charles Durang (1794–1870), who was for many years a central figure in Philadelphia's dance and theatre life. In the preface to his manual Durang states that he obtained many of the dance descriptions from teachers in Paris and London. Among the Paris masters named is Markowski, to whom Durang attributes his description of the tango.[1] The description is brief enough to include in its entirety, although the dance itself is very difficult to reconstruct and the terminology may be unfamiliar.

The Tango

The Tango was originally a South American Dance, composed in "two-fourth" time. Arranged for the ballroom, by M. Markowski.

To be danced in couples.

Part 1st—The gentleman and lady at the beginning stand face to face, without taking hands, or holding by the waist.

1. *Echappé* with the right foot, and raise the left foot; the second time to the side, point it down. Spring on the right foot slowly, the three following times quicker. The lady does the same with the gentleman.

2. Give their right hands to each other and place their left on their sides. During these steps they look under and over their arms, which they move in graceful circles four times changing their hands and feet, and finish by *Echappé levé* bringing the foot into the third position. Three *jetés,* well marked. They turn their faces from right to left, and from left to right.

The four measures which follow are different from the first [four], because the dancers turn, sometimes to the right and sometimes to the left. The Gentleman holding the lady by the waist as in the tarantular [i.e., the tarantella].

Part 2nd—Valse time movements to form the graces.

1. The gentleman takes the lady by the waist as in other dances. He commences with the left foot *coupé*, bring the left foot back slowly in the third position.

2. A *jeté* in front.

3. Aouatte (whip step) with the left foot and spring on the right foot.

4. They turn in the Valse, at their pleasure from right to left, or left to right. The gentleman commences with the right foot. The lady does the same all through taking care always to commence with the left foot, if the gentleman commences with his right or the opposite foot to the one he begins with.[2]

The musical problem arises from the instructions for the second part of the dance. Although the tango is in "two-fourth" time, according to the introductory paragraph, the second section is labeled "Valse time." At several points in his manual Durang instructs dancers to "Valse" or "Valse to places" in a dance that is not a waltz and not in waltz time. In these cases he means that they should do the step of the dance being described, but as a turning step, without altering the meter of the dance. In the tango, however, he does appear to alter the meter by taking the dancers into waltz time.

Did some tango music of the 1850s change to triple meter near the end or in some other way accommodate both "two-fourth" and waltz meters and tempi? Though I have not found any examples of this in tango music written after 1880, earlier tango songs by Sebastian Yradier (1809–65) offer some interesting possibilities.[3] The Yradier song that seems to fit best with Durang's dance description is "Maria Dolores." The earliest edition I have seen (c. 1860) was published in Madrid and bears the subtitle "Tango americano compuesto sobre un ayre habanero" (American Tango Composed on a Habanera Melody). The first sixty-seven of the song's eighty-four bars are in $\frac{2}{4}$ meter with habanera rhythm, but the last sixteen full bars are in $\frac{6}{8}$ The phrasing of the text is irregular; in fact, the shift into compound meter occurs in the middle of a text phrase. Nevertheless, the sixteen bars of $\frac{6}{8}$ (which give, in effect, thirty-two bars of waltz time) plus a chord at the end seem to fit the four phrases of "Valse-time movements" Durang requires. The transition into compound meter is easily accomplished by deriving two triplets from the pattern ♫♫♪ which mixes freely with the ♪♫♪ of the habanera.[4]

Other Yradier songs provide further evidence of the free combination of triplets and habanera patterns. "La Rubia de los lunares," a *canción habanera,* has both rhythmic patterns (♫♫♪ and ♪♫♪), the choice often dictated by the number of syllables in the text. In the instrumental interludes, however, often both halves of the bar may be in triplets. The earliest editions I have seen of both "La Paloma" and "Ay Chiquita," two other Yradier songs, are entirely in $\frac{6}{8}$.

If Yradier's songs can be taken as evidence of the significance of triple meter in early tango music, two further questions arise. First, what happened to the triplets? Why do they only appear as rhythmic accents in later tango music? I believe that triple or compound meter was easily absorbed into the more distinctive habanera rhythm as the later Argentine, French, and American dances were formed and music was composed for them. It is a simple matter to imagine several ways in which two triplets might evolve into a habanera:

Figure 5.1.

And this did happen in later French and American editions of Yradier's "La Paloma." In successive editions of "La Paloma" dating from the 1860s through about 1901, I observed a gradual ed-

Figure 5.2.

itorial process that transformed the original $\frac{6}{8}$ meter into a duple-time habanera rhythm. The music of the 1860s (Figure 5.2*a*) and that of the evolved versions available after 1900 (Figure 5.2*b*) show the beginning and end of the process.

A later French edition of "Maria Dolores" retains the mixture of ♩♩♩ ♩♩ and ♩.♩♩ ♩♩ but loses entirely the $\frac{6}{8}$ section at the end.[5] It seems possible, then, that the distinctive habanera, being identified only with the tango among the ballroom dances, took precedence over waltz time as a prominent characteristic of tango music.

The second question is whether Yradier's songs could have been a model for Markowski in choreographing the tango Durang included in his manual. Unfortunately, Markowski left no dance manual that might confirm Durang's description or tell us what music he used as his model. Yet many secondary sources attest to

Markowski's influence in the world of nineteenth-century dance, and one in particular may establish a link to Yradier's music. According to Marpon, Markowski "invented the Schottische and the Sicilienne; he imported the Mazurka to France, and many others not dignified enough to be well known. After that, he created his Friske and his Lisbonienne. It had been Mogador, the famous Mogador, that, with Christian, danced the Schottische for the first time, at the Theatre des Folies-Dramatiques."[6]

Mogador, named as the first dancer of Markowski's schottische, is Celeste Mogador (1824–1906), a celebrated dancer at the informal outdoor dance halls of mid-nineteenth-century Paris. Mogador directed an opera troupe later in her life, and she was the author of several novels, plays, and other literary works. In 1865, however, she was a cabaret singer and was known to perform Yradier's songs, including "Ay Chiquita." That she sang tango songs in the 1860s does not guarantee that Markowski knew those same songs in the 1850s; yet we know that Yradier was in Paris sometime between 1853 and 1865; hence his music was probably not unknown in that city. If Yradier's songs were models for Markowski, Mogador might have learned of them while dancing Markowski's tango.

Mogador's influence spread still further. During her days as a cabaret singer she was a close friend of Georges Bizet, and some have suggested that she might have been the model for the character of Carmen.[7] Bizet arranged an Yradier song, "El Areglito," as the now-famous habanera in *Carmen.*

Two questions remain unanswered. First is the question of tempo: if the $\frac{6}{8}$ is taken at a speed that feels waltzlike, does this destroy the integrity of the habanera? Though I have yet to find an early habanera with a tempo marking, fitting the habanera rhythm with the midcentury waltz tempo of ♩ about 144 does not seem to cause any difficulties. Second, if Markowski arranged the tango as a ballroom dance, as Durang claims, to what extent did Markowski sectionalize and separate tango and waltz steps that might have been intermixed freely by native dancers of the tango? Until we learn who these native dancers were and locate the source of Markowski's tango, this question will remain unanswered. It seems clear, however, that waltz time does have metrical significance in early tango music, and waltz time may be linked to choreographies of the dance. Ideally, further research will uncover other early descriptions of the dance that will reveal Markowski's source and provide more insight into connections between the tango and the waltz in the mid-nineteenth century.

6 The Tango in the World of Art Music

 Like most other forms of dance music, the tango moved beyond the boundaries of ballrooms, dance halls, and cabarets into the world of art music. Here, too, the most popular stereotypes assigned to characters in the tango world influenced the style and placement of tangos within larger works. And as with the waltz, the polka, the minuet, and other forms, the inclusion of a tango could help a composer evoke his or her choices of mood, atmosphere, action, and character types. Since the world of the tango involved more than a dance type and a musical form, the added factors of ennui, *mufarse,* and other images so readily available in fashionable and artistic circles seem to have resonated deeply with some composers.

Of the many examples of art music that include the tango or its cousin, the maxixe, I will examine four here.[1] Traditional analyses of each composer's works exist; hence this discussion will focus on comparing the tango in each example to stereotypes and characteristics derived from the information presented in previous chapters rather than on traditional musical analysis. Interesting aspects of such an inquiry include the intended effect of the tango's inclusion, whether that effect grew out of real or stereotyped perceptions of the tango, whether the effect was achieved in the audience's perception, whether any characteristics of the tango complemented aspects of the composer's personality or invaded the compositional process, and to what extent, by chance or design, the composer's world was connected to the world of the tango.

Erik Satie: *Sports et divertissements*

Satie composed *Sports et divertissements* in 1914, just a few years after he left the Schola Cantorum and about ten years after his deepest immersion into the world of the cafés and music halls of Montmartre. The years between 1898 and 1905, spent in and around Montmartre, placed him squarely in the world of dance music. He worked as a pianist in cafés and music halls, right in the middle of that segment of Paris which felt an immediate affinity to the characters of the early Argentine tango, and his *Trois morceaux en forme de poire* (Three Pieces in the Form of a Pear), written during this period, contains many *café-concert* melodies.

In the years around World War I, Satie composed his humorous piano pieces. Many of these had descriptive, even quirky, titles and comments spread throughout, intended solely for the amusement of the performer. Many pieces from the Renaissance to modern times have included visual, textual, or musical puns to delight the player or singer. The tango joins in that tradition with the coded meanings and secret language of Lunfardo poetry. The *Trois valses distinguées du précieux dégoûté* (Three Distinguished Waltzes of a World-Weary Dandy), from roughly the same period, contain far more verbiage than *Sports et divertissements,* and the third waltz (all of them describe a worldly sophisticate) refers to dancing the fashionable dances of the day—which, of course, included the tango. Each of the twenty miniature pieces in *Sports et divertissements* is accompanied by a few words and a drawing, combining the composer's text, music, and calligraphy into a whole that makes its public performance of necessity incomplete for everyone except the performer. This idea, that no matter what is presented to the public there is nonetheless more (not better or deeper, just more), suggests the image of the introspective tango dancer who gives away only what he chooses, to whom he chooses.

Sports et divertissements as Satie completed it has outlasted its original intent, which was to accent an album picturing a variety of pastimes. Ironically, Stravinsky first turned down the commission because the fee was too low; Satie initially rejected it because it was too high. Eventually a suitably low fee was offered, and Satie took on the project.[2] Also ironic is the fact that Satie's work was so exquisite that at first only a deluxe edition was published, high priced and available to only a very limited audience.

Perhaps the verbal element that best connects Satie to the thoughts and feelings of the tango is found in the preface. Satie writes:

> This publication is made up of two artistic elements: drawing, music. The drawing part is represented by strokes—strokes of wit; the musical part is depicted by dots—black dots. These two parts together—in a single volume—form a whole; an album. I advise the reader to leaf through this book with a friendly and benevolent hand, for it is a work of fantasy. No more should be read into it.
>
> For the Stunted and the Stupid I have written a serious and respectable Choral. It is a sort of bitter preamble, a kind of austere and unfrivolous introduction.
>
> I have put into it all I know about Boredom. I dedicate this choral to those who do not like me. I withdraw.[3]

Several of these ideas could have been written by Contursi, Arolas, or others from Argentina. The bitterness, the separation from those the composer considers stupid and unworthy, the dismissive toss of boredom at the face of respectability—all fit well into the struggles of tango composers to have their work understood.

Yet one must not make too much of these possible connections to the tango, partly because such a lack of subtlety is anathema to the tango itself. Also, such feelings of boredom and bitterness as Satie expresses existed equally well before the tango was invented. *Sports et divertissements* stands on its own. Its twenty pieces cover a range of humorous emotions and situations, and the tango is not the only dance rhythm used.

Three dance pieces are loosely connected: "Le pique-nique" uses a polka, "Le water-chute" uses a valse-musette, and the "Tango perpétuel" completes the trio. They are linked into an account of the events of a day trip. The tango lives up to its title by being the only one of the twenty pieces intended to be repeated. Performance instructions are that the piece is to be played *modéré et très ennuyé* (moderately and with great boredom), a perfect description of the mannerism adopted by Parisian dancers enthralled with the tango. The accompanying text serves as the epigraph to this chapter.

Despite its brevity, the "Tango perpetual" shows the composer's familiarity with a surprising number of characteristics found in Argentine tangos. Although there are no bar lines (typical of Satie's compositional style), a steady rhythm is maintained through a simple, strict, repetitive habanera in the left-hand part. The habanera is constructed with a dotted-eighth-note b, a sixteenth-note c (which may or may not be sharped), and e and c as the two final eighth notes, respectively. Other than an octave ascent for the last four statements of the pattern, the habanera is unchanging. In the right hand Satie compresses a number of typical tango patterns into a small space. He includes the later variation on the habanera that uses a sixteenth note, an eighth note, another sixteenth note, and two final eighth notes. He also uses quick ornamental sixteenth-note triplets, rocking passages of sixteenth notes centered within a narrow range, parallel melodies, and the division of the habanera between a sustained note melody and a rhythmically active line. All of these techniques have been identified in popular tangos of the day, although few composers managed to use so many choices to such advantage in a single piece.

Example 6.1. Types of tango melodies in Erik Satie's "Tango perpétuel": (*a*) ornamental sixteenth-note triplets; (*b*) sixteenth notes within a narrow range; (*c*) parallel melody; (*d*) division of the habanera between two rhythmically disparate lines.

Darius Milhaud: *Le bœuf sur le toit*

Music publishers in the United States and Europe often blurred the distinctions between different kinds of dance music, advertising pieces as usable for more than one type of dance. A frequent pairing was the tango and the Brazilian maxixe, and pieces were variously labeled tango, maxixe, tango-maxixe, tango bresilienne, Brazilian tango, Brazilian tango—two-step, maxixe bresilienne, or tango—maxixe—two-step. In looking at pieces of art music labeled as or resembling either tango or maxixe, one must consider where the composer would most likely have formed his impressions of each form.

Milhaud's *Le bœuf sur le toit* (1919) predates the composer's exposure to jazz, but it coincides with his membership in Les Six and follows his two years in Brazil as secretary to the French minister. Native Brazilian music and atmosphere made a strong impression on Milhaud; thus his inclusion of the maxixe in *Le bœuf* grows out of firsthand experience with the original character of this dance music. That Milhaud learned about the maxixe in Brazil is important in light of the difference in style between the native Brazilian and Paris cabaret versions. In the fantasia he entitled *Le bœuf sur le toit* he included popular tangos, maxixes, sambas, and other Hispanic dances, intermixing them with a recurring theme. The title of this work comes from a Brazilian popular song. Milhaud's original idea was that this music might serve as the accompaniment to a Charlie Chaplin silent film. Poet Jean Cocteau had other ideas, however, and created a pantomime that would fit with the music. In his memoir, Milhaud describes Cocteau's plot:

> He imagined a scene in a bar in America during Prohibition. The various characters were highly typical: a Boxer, a Negro Dwarf, a Lady of Fashion, a Red-Headed Woman dressed as a man, a Bookmaker, a Gentleman in evening clothes. The Barman, with a face like that of Antinoüs, offers everyone cocktails. After a few incidents and various dances, a Policeman enters, whereupon the scene is immediately transformed into a milk-bar. The clients play a rustic scene and dance a pastourale as they sip glasses of milk. The Barman switches on a big fan, which decapitates the Policeman. The Redheaded Woman executes a dance with the Policeman's head, ending by standing on her hands like the Salome in Rouen Cathedral. One by one the customers drift away, and the Barman presents an enormous bill to the resuscitated Policeman.

Several aspects of this plot have correspondences in the world of the tango and, by association, of the maxixe. A bar during Prohibition—in other words, a bar to which respectable people would not go—is a typical setting in the tango world. Nearly all the characters, with the possible exception of the Lady of Fashion, fit with the character types associated with the tango—all that is missing is a *compadrito*—even though the tradition of female tango singers dressing as men did not develop until the late 1920s.

Despite Milhaud's legitimate connection to Brazilian music, French audiences saw Milhaud's use of maxixe and other South American rhythms as evidence of his taste for whatever was odd or novel. *Le bœuf* premiered in a program that also included works by Satie, Auric, and Poulenc. Milhaud's recollection of the response to this program speaks for itself:

> The lighthearted show, presented under the aegis of Erik Satie and treated by the newspapers as a practical joke, was regarded by the public as symbolizing the music-hall and circus system of aesthetics . . . both public and critics agreed that I was a clown and a strolling musician—I, who hated comedy and in composing *Le bœuf sur le toit* had only aspired to create a merry, unpretentious divertissement in memory of the Brazilian rhythms that had so captured my imagination and never—no, never!—made me laugh.[4]

Of course, one must place some of the blame for Milhaud's disappointment on Cocteau and his odd pantomime, but the music-hall connection was to haunt Milhaud for a long time. *Le bœuf* received much the same response in London, where it was performed at the Coliseum, London's largest music hall. Coliseum audiences were unfazed by extremely diverse programs, although the musicians found the score somewhat daunting. Audience response was summarized for Milhaud in the overheard words of one London workman: "It ain't that it makes you laugh; but it's different, see, so it makes you laugh!"[5]

In *Le bœuf sur le toit*, Milhaud uses elements of tango and maxixe quite freely. The lower instruments, which generally carry the habanera, use both simple and ornamented versions of this rhythm. Only occasionally is the customary melodic pattern, which encloses an ascending octave, used for any length of time. Often the bass lines are chromatic or follow interval patterns that create more rapid modulations than would be found in a traditional tango or maxixe. Milhaud creates somewhat longer segments of the distinctive maxixe bass line, in which the third note of the habanera rhythm descends to the lower octave. Also particular to the maxixe is the creation of a polka rhythm of an eighth note and two sixteenth notes, distributed between the lower and upper strings, and appearing in recurring episodes. Popular South American tunes and their accompanying material are found in the higher voices. The combination of the various dance types is more an evocation of their styles than a direct insertion of each one. Multiple variations on traditional rhythms occur within a more condensed space, and much of the accompanying material is more complex than one would ordinarily find in dance music of this time period. All of this is, of course, perfectly consistent with Milhaud's intention to create an unpretentious memory of South America rather than to write a tango or maxixe within a larger work.

William Walton: *Façade*

Walton first envisioned his *Façade* as an entertainment to be performed at the home of his friends and sometime patrons, the Sitwells. Edith Sitwell's experimental nonsense poetry, designed to create fleeting images through rhyme and rhythm rather than to form a cohesive text, was to be accompanied by short pieces composed by Walton. The texts were to be declaimed rhythmically on a single pitch by a single voice, preferably devoid of expression or emotion. The staging was simple but startling: on a curtain, an enormous head with a gigantic mouth was fitted with a megaphone for the reciter's use. Walton was able to make several clever points of connection between quotations of music-hall songs and corresponding words from the songs that appeared in

Sitwell's texts. Thus far the connections to the tango are that both shared the option of obscure poetry and the venue of the music hall—although since Walton was a friend of artistic, upper-class Britons and earned money arranging music for jazz bands, it is likely that he was reasonably familiar with the tango and other popular modern dance genres.

Façade's second incarnation was as one or two orchestral suites, and in its final rearrangement it became a ballet score. I will examine the "Tango-Pasodoble" from the first orchestral suite here. This work is in three large sections. Walton's scoring is quite similar to popular orchestrations of tangos. The habanera, whether ornamented or simple, is divided among the strings and most often follows the traditional ascending and descending line no matter what intervals are chosen. Frank Howes has identified two music-hall tunes in the "Tango-Pasodoble." The first is an explicit statement of "I Do Like to Be Beside the Seaside" by the cor anglais, and the second is a possible allusion to "Get Out and Get Under the Automobile."[6] The second tune serves as a brief prelude to the return of "Seaside" in the third section of the piece.

The habanera in the first section eventually disintegrates, and all voices join in a chromatic modulation from $E^\flat$ to G. Neither chromaticism nor third-related modulations are unusual in tangos of the 1920s, but Walton's modulation is more linear than harmonic, something not seen for several more years in the popular music world of the tango. The second section drops the habanera altogether but still assigns the supporting rhythmic structure to the string section. It now shares elements of an oompah bass such as one might find supporting a polka or a marchlike pasodoble. The chromatic element continues in the accompanying voices, and a melody in popular style in dotted notes, fragmented and played in parallel intervals, appears in the woodwinds. The modulation back to $E^\flat$ for the third section is more abrupt, pivoting on the common note G. Again the cor anglais has the tune, this time doubled by a solo violin. The rest of the string section again creates the habanera by dividing the rhythm pattern. When the "Sea-side" tune returns, it is given to the trombone. This time new, fast triplet flourishes in the habanera, coupled with the addition of castanets, give a feeling more Spanish than Argentine.

It is appropriate that Walton's "Tango-Pasodoble" is included within a piece called *Façade.* It is difficult to tell whether the tango rhythms, flourishes, and orchestration form the façade for the music-hall tunes or whether popular melodies cover the inherent qualities of the tango.

Ernst Křenek: *Jonny spielt auf*

Scandal mixed with enthusiasm was the response to Křenek's 1926 opera *Jonny spielt auf*—the same response that had greeted the tango upon its arrival in Paris. Several threads of Křenek's life during the mid-1920s mirror themes from the tango world. By this time Křenek was known as a composer with two very distinct sides, one highly comic and one highly pedantic. The themes of separation from a woman (specifically, his divorce from Anna Mahler) and the search for sympathetic friends, while not unique to the tango world, are strong within it. In addition, the mid-1920s saw Křenek in a state of melancholia: he was unable to respond to congenial surroundings, stimulating company, or offers of meaningful work, and he began to suffer financial hardship—a condition not unlike the tango's state of *mufarse.* It took two offers of work with the state opera company in Kassel to nudge him back into activity. Despite the cool reception Kassel audiences had given Křenek's earlier works, he needed the job. During the summer of 1925, as he learned about theatre and prepared to take up his new position in Kassel, Křenek also made considerable progress on *Jonny spielt auf.* Even the shift into relative prosperity that came with the new job resembles a tango theme: a wealthy female patron, Emy Rubensohn, saved Křenek from life in a lonely single room. Through her influence and support he found a better place to live, and a world of social and artistic contacts opened up. In the words of biographer John L. Stewart, "He was not happy, but he was no longer so dreadfully alone."[7]

The subscription series at the Kassel opera house included a variety of works, but the audience had a decided preference for traditional or antimodernist productions. Křenek's vaguely defined duties included composing background music for new productions, conducting small-scale concerts of traditional works, and writing program notes. In addition, the opportunity to learn the latest techniques of production and staging contributed a great deal to the creation of *Jonny spielt auf.*

A love of trains and an enthusiastically received introduction to jazz also contributed to the images Křenek chose in telling the story of Jonny. The spark that led to the completion of *Jonny* was Křenek's attendance at Chocolate Kiddies, a jazz revue of 1926 performed by an all—African American troupe. Like many Europeans at this time, Křenek had seen and heard of African Americans but had never met one. Stereotypes and images such as that of Josephine Baker marked his perception. His understanding of jazz was completely external. Nonetheless, these two encounters represented for Křenek the exuberance and newness of American life. John Stewart describes Křenek's attitude toward African Americans:

> He had no idea that "nigger-boy," which he borrowed, as other German speakers did, from English, was a humiliating term. Nor did he perceive that those who professed to envy black people for their spontaneity, their childlike directness, and their unselfconscious exuberance were patronizing them. He really meant it when he said that he passionately desired the fullness of life that he embodied in *Jonny.* He was not and never would be a racist.[8]

If Stewart's characterization of Křenek is accurate, then race is not a signifier in considering Jonny's relationship to tango themes, even though race was a determining factor in class assignment in

Argentina and a motivation for many conflicts played out in the tango.

Irrespective of their race, Křenek's characters resemble their counterparts within the tango paradigm. Jonny, leaving aside his musical abilities for the moment, is the embodiment of the early *compadrito*—the wisecracking, good-natured, exuberant petty thief who skirts the action but influences the fate of everyone in his sphere. In Max, the composer, one can see the isolated, brooding tango composers, immersed in their own suffering and, of course, betrayed by their women. The singer Anita—for naturally there must be a fickle woman in a tango scenario—is victim or betrayer, depending on one's gender bias in interpreting the events of the opera. The fourth character, Daniello, is a rival *compadrito,* competing with Jonny for the violin and with Max for the woman. Křenek builds a tango world not only in the characters themselves but also in the ways they affect and interact with each other. And at the moment when all their lives intertwine—when the *compadritos* seduce and steal, the woman gives in and betrays, and the suffering artist loses all—almost the entire paradigm of the tango is played out. It is here, by chance or design, that Křenek places the musical tango in *Jonny spielt auf.*

The essentials of plot and characters could be set in Buenos Aires with so little effort that it is tempting to assume Křenek knew all about the early characters of the tango world. That is not likely, nor was it Křenek's intent. He saw the conflict as being more between the West (United States) and the East (Europe), and between the Old Order (represented by the European establishment and the introspection of Max) and the New Order (represented by the liveliness, optimism, and freedom of Jonny, jazz, and the new kinds of dancing). Most likely he chose a tango for the so-called seduction scene just because the tango was a fashionable metaphor for seduction. Yet, as with most successful paradigms for human emotion, the tango's truest meanings are universal and can easily be found outside its own world.

Křenek heard Paul Whiteman's orchestra while he was composing *Jonny spielt auf,* and he was impressed by the size and scope of sound the orchestra provided, in comparison to what he knew already of Palm Court—style dance bands. Although Whiteman played little jazz, the sound of his orchestra represented for Křenek the latest trends in American popular music. Thus, little real jazz is used in the opera. Flatted thirds in melody lines serve as blues, and dotted rhythms are meant to be played as written, without the flexible, improvised quality of real jazz.[9] That *Jonny* was billed as a jazz opera all the way through is evidence of how little sophistication European opera audiences had about what really defined jazz.

German audiences loved *Jonny spielt auf.* The scandalous sexual escapades, the intriguing special effects (such as the giant locomotive that removes Daniello at just the right moment, and the slapstick physical action reminiscent of contemporary films), and the fashionable music that passed for jazz were new and different enough to ensure success, despite the high moral tone of the predominantly negative reviews. The mistake was in staging *Jonny* in New York and Paris, where bad text translations brought laughter from the audience and where listeners, who were constantly exposed to real jazz and real African American performers, found the music silly and ridiculed European concepts of jazz. In addition, although Křenek's original conception of Jonny as an African American was not motivated by conscious racial bigotry, events at the New York staging made race a focal point. At the Met the character of Jonny, as well as other characters of African descent, had to be performed by singers in blackface. Much of the audience's ridicule was because this change was reflected only in the printed text of the libretto, not in the sung text. This gave race a significance Křenek had not intended and added a level of societal disapproval to the interracial relationship between Jonny and Anita. One is reminded of *Justicia criolla,* the Argentine *sainete* in which the tango is used to play out the tensions caused by a similar inter-racial relationship. Few performances of *Jonny* were given out-side Germany, and everyone, including Křenek, was soon bored with the whole thing. Only in modern revival has it been staged again with success.[10]

The tango in *Jonny spielt auf* takes place as Daniello rescues Anita from Jonny, then seduces her. Meanwhile, Jonny, who has a plan of his own, observes the action. The scene ends with Daniello and Anita retiring to her room and Jonny making plans to steal Daniello's valuable violin. The text assigns what one might con-sider the romantic aspects of seduction to a chorus, and an off-stage jazz band plays the music. Daniello and Jonny urge Anita to listen to the chorus's seduction song. Anita's textual response is to melt, based on the fact that she finds Daniello handsome.

When one has studied the tangos of Villoldo, Arolas, Firpo, and others, it is fair to say that Křenek's musical conception of a tango has little to recommend it. His use of habanera is consistent with late-1920s practice; that is, it is not always present, nor is it confined to the lower voices. He uses the ornamented version of the habanera (a sixteenth note, an eighth, another sixteenth, and a quarter or two eighths to finish the pattern) as often as he uses the simpler traditional pattern. Only at the end of the tango sec-tion, which is an instrumental coda, does the habanera dominate the bass line. Variations on fragments of habanera rhythms are chosen with a good ear for text setting. The melodies themselves seem almost randomly chromatic, however, and the vocal lines combine rather ungracefully Křenek's limited understanding of the nature of dance music with something of the style of art-song melody in the 1920s. The same can be said of the harmony. Were it not for the quality of the other jazz music, the tango might have been successful as a self-parody. As it is, the music actually con-tains the weakest link to the world of the tango. Yet, of the four examples studied here, the characters of Křenek's tango come the closest to fitting the tango paradigm. That they do so by chance and because they fit those themes of the tango that are universal is an interesting irony.

The appearance of the tango in art music is not in itself surprising. Composers of art music have always used dance styles in a variety of ways and for a variety of reasons. Use of the tango is of special interest because its scandalous period coincided so closely with its period of greatest popularity as a social dance and because its exotic character types were available to dancers, musicians, and composers to convey whatever meaning or metaphor they chose. Nonetheless, even those composers who encountered the tango in its earliest Parisian years most likely learned only of the stereotyped emotions and characters quickly adopted by the cabaret and dance crowd. One can only regret the richness of expression for which the tango might have served if composers of art music had known its whole history.

Appendix 1. Tango Steps, 1911–1925

Glossary

Ballroom position (also called **waltz position**). Partners are face to face, usually backing the woman in line of direction. He has his right arm around her waist, her left hand is on his shoulder, and his left hand holds her right hand slightly out to the side.

First foot. Usually the man's left and the woman's right in ragtime dance repertoire. However, in the tango sources this is often reversed, and the man's right foot and the woman's left are the first feet. The opposite foot is called the second foot. Most promenade and ballroom steps have partners starting on opposite feet; most skaters' steps start on the same feet.

Line of direction (also called **line of dance**). The common direction in which all couples progress around a ballroom, usually counterclockwise.

Over-the-shoulders position. A reverse promenade in which the handhold remains the same but partners are looking away from their clasped hands (the woman looks over her left shoulder and the man looks over his right shoulder). Dancers can move in or against line of direction.

Promenade position. Both partners face forward in line of direction, standing side by side, usually holding hands as in ballroom position.

Skaters' position. Partners are side by side using a variety of handholds, such as holding left hands in front to the left side, and right hands behind on the woman's right hip.

Explanatory Notes

1. Unless otherwise specified, when steps are given only for the man, it is assumed the woman does the step using the opposite feet, and often in the opposite direction.

2. Spellings of step names vary considerably from source to source, and there are often errors in the choices of articles when the name is not in the writer's native language. Also, there is no consistent way to list steps. Some give their catalog using only the step names, while others use a variety of spellings for first, second, third, etc., when listing steps by a numbering system. In this appendix, each source's spellings, usages of foreign terms, and numberings of lists have been preserved in order to provide further evidence of the variety and lack of standardization in Europe and the United States.

3. Descriptions of steps have been interpreted, simplified, and paraphrased. When a step name such as *rueda,* grapevine, or *media luna* appears as part of the description, a definition of that step can be found at the end of chapter 2.

4. Rhythms are not always included in the source description of a step. Where they are specified, or where the rhythm is discernible from the step itself or in correlation with similar steps, rhythm patterns are given by means of the letter Q and S, representing quick and slow steps, respectively. Typically, a slow step takes exactly twice as much time as a quick step.

5. Most sources give several steps in the tango repertoire. The most common instruction, such as that given by Maurice Mouvet,[1] is for dancers to use the descriptions as a menu, putting the steps together in whatever sequence seems best to them, and paying attention to beginning and ending phrases with such appropriate steps as the *corte.* A few writers, such as Caroline Walker,[2] give their steps in an order that can be used as a sequence, and some others, such as F. L. Clendenen,[3] give a menu of steps and follow it with some sample choreographies for ballroom or stage.

Sources

See: United States, United Kingdom, France, Germany, Italy and Spain

United States

Sheafe, Alfonso. *The Fascinating Boston.* Boston: Boston Music Company, 1913.

1. Mouvet, *The Tango,* 11.
2. Walker, *Modern Dances,* 11–12.
3. Clendenen, *Dance Mad,* 9 ff.

Tango No. 1. Partners take ballroom position, with the difference that the man's left hand holds the woman's right hand to his left shoulder. Back the man one step, starting back left for him. Follow with two cross steps in the same direction. Then a half turn "in the same direction" (ambiguous?). Four measures of the two-step (a polka without a hop), and repeat the whole as many times as the couple wishes.

Tango No. 2. Start in the same position as Tango No. 1. Very slow box step, begin backing the man on his left two steps, then his side left two steps, two steps forward, and two steps to his right. [Sheafe does not specify the last two steps, but says that the whole takes eight measures and returns to the original position by moving in the opposite direction from the first four measures.] To finish, the couple does eight measures of two-step. The whole figure can be repeated at will.

Castle, Vernon, and Irene Castle. *Modern Dancing.* New York: Harper and Brothers, 1914.

Cortez. After backing the woman, the man steps back left, back right, side left, and back right (SQQS).

Media luna. Step forward right (S), then forward left and replace left with right (QQ). Then back left (S), and back right and replace it with the left (QQ).

Scissors. From a promenade walk, partners turn to face and step across their own feet, twisting back and forth.

Promenade. In promenade position, walk forward on first foot 1, 2. On count three & turn in to face partner and step side-close. Return to promenade and continue the pattern, which crosses the musical beat.

El Charron. Walk and turn in right shoulder Yale (partners face opposite directions, side by side touching right shoulders, usually with hands in ballroom position).

The Ring. *Rueda* with *corte.*

Tango *volta.* Ordinary waltz step done very slowly.

Eight Step. Walk in promenade; every third count, the person on the left side walks in front, changing sides. Move in line of direction, alternating between promenade and over-the-shoulders positions.

Innovation. All steps done without partners touching.

Clendenen, F. Leslie. *Dance Mad; Or, the Dances of the Day.* St. Louis: Arcade, 1914.

Stage Tango

Step 1. Forward left, right, left; close right with one-quarter turn; repeat to make a square.

Step 2. Very slow steps, four forward and four backward.

Step 3. Promenade position: Forward left, right, left, dip and turn toward partner, reverse in opposite direction. Face partner on count four; four counts of rocking *molinete.*

Step 4. "Tangle Foot." Face partner; cross left in front, uncross right and point, reverse, then cross left, point, cross right, point (scissors).

Step 5. Sweep left, then right behind (SS), dip back on left (S), shift forward and close (QQ), forward left (S).

Step 6. Scorpion draws to left side, then turn around partner.

Step 7. "Military." Supposedly an Argentine step. In promenade position. Forward left, right, point left toe forward and twist toward partner, raising heel. Turn back to line of direction and repeat.

Step 8. Slide left forward, right forward, sweep left around and across right. Step on right, dip forward left, step forward right, back left, shift forward right.

Step 9. Stamp forward left, hop on right, hold two more counts. Do this alternately, moving around partner.

Step 10. In skaters' position; walk backward and forward with dips on each count four.

Step 11. Keep right crossed in front, move sideways in line of direction, keep hands raised to shoulder height.

Step 12. Rocking *molinete,* forward left, back right.

Step 13. Eight counts grapevine, four counts turning around partner, two counts deep dips forward, repeat.

Step 14. The man holds the woman's right hand behind her back. She turns away, pivots out, kneels on right knee for two counts. She rises, turns back into position. Back the man with slow steps.

Step 15. Promenade position. Right hands raised, walk forward left, right, back left and close right, forward left (SSQQS), repeat.

Step 16. Turn around partner, dipping with knee to the floor on count seven, rise on count eight.

Step 17. Cross left over right, then right over left, alternating with rhythm SSQQQQ (scissors?).

Step 18. Man facing in, do a grapevine starting crossing in front with the left. Always cross in front.

Step 19. Promenade position: forward left, right, left, turn to over-the-shoulders position, dipping on counts three and four. Forward left, dip, rise and dip again, swing right through and return to original direction.

Step 20. In promenade, forward left, right and dip, twist one-half around, twist back, pivoting woman under raised arm. Repeat three times to make a circle.

Step 21. Single three. Promenade forward left, cross right in front, short step back left, kicking right.

There follow six choreographed tangos using the above steps.

Argentine Tango

Corte No. 1. Forward right, left, close right, and back left, point left forward.

Corte No. 2. Forward right, touch left forward, sweep left back and forth, forward left.

Corte No. 3. Forward right, side left, rise and descend, weight on left, point right forward.

El Corte coupe, Corte No. 4. Forward right, close left in front, cut under with right and flick left, circle left back into corte and hold.

Le Corte No. 5. Forward right, side left and close right, back left and hold.

El Corte No. 6. Forward right, left, circle back right, circle back left, repeat starting forward left.

Le Corte No. 7. Forward right, left, back right, back left.

Le Corte No. 8. Forward right, point side left and close in first position, slightly raise right.

El Medio corte. Back right, side left (toe up), pivot out, back left.

Circa. Rueda. On count seven, step forward right; on count eight, point forward left.

Carre (Square). Cross right in front, side left, cross right in front, turn one-quarter right and step side left, side right, cross left in front, side right, turn one-quarter right with side left; repeat, starting cross right in front.

Cruzado con corte. Cross right in front, close left with weight, stamp right. Reverse for counts three and four. The woman does scissors around the man.

Corte con quebrado. Promenade position. Cross right in front, circling, then left over right. Continue alternating going around in a circle.

El Cruzado. Forward right; twist one-half around, keeping feet in fourth position; turn back to line of direction, circling forward left, back right.

Les Ciseaux. Cross right in front, side left, cross right in front, point side left, twisting right, reverse. (This is a double; the single is cross, point, cross, point, etc.)

Le Huit croise. Forward left, cross right in front, uncross left, dip, back right, cross left in front, uncross right, dip.

Huit croise (Twinkle). Forward right, close left, back right, forward left, close right, back left.

La Marche. Back the woman four steps.

La Media luna No. 18. Forward right and box.

La Media luna No. 19. Forward right, left, right, side left (with possible half turn), close right. Walk.

La Media luna No. 20. Forward right, left, cut right under left, back left, back right, forward left.

La Media luna No. 21, Forward right, close left, forward right (QQS), then back.

Media luna No. 22. Forward right, sweep and cross over (QQS).

El Paseo. Back the woman. On count eight, side left and point right to the side. Repeat backwards.

El Paseo de lado No. 25. Back the lady, half turn, back the man.

El Paseo de lado No. 25a. Alternating grapevine.

El Paseo No. 26. Slow walk, dropping heel on second beat.

Paseo con golpe. Cross right in front, then left in front, stamp right behind and raise left, point side left, drop left heel, *corte.*

El Ocho. Walk, walk, the man pivots in front; walk, walk, the woman pivots in front of the man.

Las Tijeras. Cross right, uncross left, cross right, point left, reverse. Single: cross right, uncross and point left, cross left, uncross and point right.

La Rueda No. 30. Cross right over left, left over right, right over left, unwind, reverse. End with *corte.*

La Rueda No. 31. Cross right over left, the woman chassés around. Pause on last count.

The Fan. Double and Single Scissors, with the addition that on the points, the heel is raised even with the knee.

Le Ronde. Cross right behind, uncross side left, close right, point left side, reverse. The woman crosses forward to begin.

La Promenade. Forward right, left, close right, forward left, hold.

Tap Step. Back the woman four steps, then promenade counts five and six, tap heels forward and at the side.

Volteo. Alternating grapevine, beginning with the man crossing right behind.

Open Walk. Forward right, point left back, forward left, point right back, four counts for a half turn, then repeat, backing the man.

Tango. Forward right, forward left on toe, close right and one-half turn, back left, point right forward.

Half-time Step. Promenade position: forward right, left (SS), repeat with dips.

Back right, left, right, left, repeat, ending with Tango step.

Corkscrew: Waltz or Promenade position. Cross left in front, cross right in front (SS), keep crossing once per beat (Qs—perhaps QQQQ), repeat twice.

El Golpeado. Back the woman four steps, stamp right heel, side right, stamp side left, stamp beside right, repeat.

Clendenen also includes a *Parisienne Tango* choreography, and quotes Barrassa's steps, which appear later in this appendix in S. Beach Chester's collection.

Hopkins, J. S. *The Tango and Other Up-to-Date Dances.* Chicago: Saalfield, 1914.

Step 1. Ballroom position, walking two steps per bar, ending with a double corte.

Step 2. Pomander (or Yale) turn, pointing toes of the free foot to the side at the end of the phrase.

Step 3. Straight walking with quarter turns.

Catch Step: Walking in promenade position, with a *chassé* or step/close on counts 2 &.

Bend Step: Walking in promenade position, with a forward dip on count two.

Minuet Step: Right hands together down to the elbows, circle turn and reverse.

Grapevine: Side step and cross step, partners crossing opposite.

Interlude: Swing turn and stepped turn.

Santley #2: Walking in promenade, partners exchange places on count three, so that in the first measure, the woman is on the man's right side, and in the second measure the man is on the woman's right side.

Slow Step: Promenade SSQQ (changing sides on the quicks), point the leading feet on count four.

Step and Step Bend: Promenade walk on counts one through five, dip on count six, change direction on seven, point the feet on count eight.

Grapevine Turn: Four counts grapevine, four counts turning.

At this point Hopkins includes more steps, but several times starts the numbering over again with a new Step 1.

Step 1: Walking steps, turning left on every count four.

Step 2: Like Step 1, but backing the man instead of the woman.

Step 3: Cross second foot (right for the man, left for the woman), over, then sweep first foot around while turning toward partner.

Step 4: Dipping promenade with *media luna,* repeat in reverse promenade (over-the-shoulders position).

Step 5: Walk and dip.

Criss-Cross: Grapevine, holding arms out to the side.

Step 1: Back the man. On count eight &, he turns to the woman's right (backs to the outside), and continues in an over-the-shoulders promenade.

Step 2: Over-the-shoulders promenade, then the woman switches sides to continue in a normal promenade.

Step 3: In promenade, point forward walk, walk, close.

Step 4: In promenade, walk, walk, *media luna.*

Step 5: After Step 4's *media luna,* turn back, step across with first foot (to over-the-shoulder), step, step, point.

Step 6: Step 5, done on opposite feet.

Step 7: Promenade, walk, walk, pivot, pivot, repeat.

Includes a description of the innovation (a method created by Vernon Castle for dancing the tango without touching one's partner).

Miller, Stanley. *The Tango as Danced in the Ballroom.* N.p.: George Anderson, 1914 (pamphlet).

No. 1. Back the man five steps.

No. 2. (half reverse). The man steps side right and closes.

No. 3. Back the woman five steps.

No. 4. A full reverse in place.

No. 5. Grapevine, opposite crosses.

Mouvet, Maurice. *The Tango and the New Dances.* Chicago: Laird and Lee, 1914.

The Walk: Back the man [Mouvet says that the man starts on his right foot and the woman on her left].

Corte: The man steps back right, touches left to right and returns left to place, steps back left into *corte* position, holds for count four.

El Paseo: A *rueda,* the man crosses right over left.

The Single Three: The man steps forward left, crosses right in front, uncrosses left to close with right (QQS).

The Fan: A possible misprint here: Mouvet wants the dancers to cross feet and pivot, repeating. His use of rights and lefts is ambiguous.

Scissors: Apparently two small *ruedas.*

Newman, Albert W. *Dances of To-day.* Philadelphia: Penn, 1914.

The Tango Step: Slow, gliding walk backing the woman, two steps per measure. Two steps backing the woman, then point the left forward, turn to face partner and raise right heel. On count four, drop the right heel and face line of direction. Repeat in line of direction, or turning right at the end of each sequence. The woman steps opposite.

The Square: At one corner, facing out of a square, step side left, cross right in front, and uncross left behind, turning one quarter right. Facing into the square, to move along the next side, step side right, cross left in front, uncross right behind, again turning one quarter right. Facing out of the square, repeat to finish the last two sides of the square. The woman steps opposite, but crosses like the man.

Walk Out: Use the tango step for unused music in a phrase.

Double Overlapping Step (Scissors Step): The man crosses left in front, uncrosses side right, recrosses left front, points side right, reverse. Woman steps opposite.

Two-Step and Bend: Two-step to the side. Cross free foot behind, dip, and uncross, pointing free foot to side.

Cross Dip Step: Join hands with partner, hold arms straight out (i.e., "Airplane position"). Side step with first foot, cross second foot in front, dip with weight on second foot. Raise the man's left and the woman's right hands overhead, repeat to the other side.

Single Over-lapping Step: (Scissors Step): Cross first foot in front, uncross second foot, point it to the side, cross second foot in front, uncross first foot, point it to the side. Continue.

The Fan: In promenade position, walk forward three steps starting on the first foot. On count three, dip forward on the first foot and rock weight back onto the second foot. Repeat. Then point the first foot forward, to the side, behind, and to the side again.

El Corte (or *Pas d'arret* or stop step). The man steps back right, side left, close right, back left, hold (SQQS-).

El Marcha: Back the woman, taking three slow steps and holding on the second beat of the second measure.

El Paseo: A slow walk, taking one step per measure.

El Chase: Step forward on the second foot, do a two-step, then a step forward on the first foot (rhythm is SQQS). (If the man is backing the woman, the two-step is done to the side. If in promenade position, the dancers quickly face each other for the two-step.)

Newman gives names of more Argentine steps, describing their general appearance without including usable instructions. He also includes seven very brief tango sequences made up from these steps.

Walker, Caroline. *The Modern Dances: How to Dance Them.* Chicago: Saul Brothers, 1914.

One-Step Tango

4 Steps: Back the woman, then back the man.

Circling: Pomander (or Yale) turn, four steps, reverse direction for four steps.

Grapevine: Side-Cross, partners cross on opposite feet; feet do not completely cross.

Draw: Slow side-close (dragging the trailing foot closed), bending bodies to the side.

Criss-Cross: Skaters' grapevine.

4 Step Grapevine: Four grapevine steps, quarter turn, repeat, to make a square.

Grapevine Dip: Dip on the crossing step of the grapevine.

Shuffle: Six steps in promenade, turn in, six steps in opposite direction.

Lame Duck: Promenade, dipping forward on the first foot.

Walker also includes several combinations suggesting ways to link the above steps together into longer sequences.

Argentine Tango

4 Steps: Walk, backing the man.

1st Figure: Four steps in promenade, bend, turn and hold on counts five through eight, repeat.

2nd Figure: In promenade. Step, dip, face partner, point forward with outside foot.

3rd Figure: Promenade four steps. Count five: turn to partner; count six: point second foot in opposite direction.

4th Figure (Scissors): Promenade on second foot; walk counts one to four. On five pivot toward partner, step in opposite direction with second foot, and brush first foot back. On six and seven, step against line of direction, repeat pivot and brush on eight.

Circle: A *rueda*. The man crosses right over left.

Single *Cortez:* The man walks backward on counts one and two (ending count two with a brush of the foot), and *cortes* forward on count three, holding on four.

Double *Cortez:* Single *corte* without touching partner, repeat three more times.

Mouvet, Maurice. *The Art of Dancing.* New York: Schirmer, 1915.

Promenade: Back the woman four steps (in ballroom position).

Half *cortez:* Forward right, point left on counts two and three, step back left on count four.

Pas *chassez:* Forward right and left, point right forward diagonally, close right to left.

Media luna: Forward right and left, draw right to left.

Cortez: Forward right and left (QQ), close right to left on count two, step forward left and hold.

Chassez: Three diagonal side-close steps, clicking heels.

Single Three: Back the man three steps, close with heel clicks.

Scissors: Both partners step back and forth across their own feet, presumably moving toward each other.

Cruz, C. *The Modern Ballroom Tango.* U.S.A.: n.p., 1925.

The March: Forward right, backing the woman on counts one through four, then pause. The woman can cross right behind on count four.

The Half Turn: Forward left, turning, shift back right, cross left over right, back right turning, cross left in front, close right with weight. (Her cross means crossing right behind left. Use reverse waltz turn.)

The Lace Step: Side left, cross right in front, continue in a grapevine, the woman crosses opposite.

The Promenade: Walk, walk, face partner, side-close (SSQQ).

Note: End with a rotation to repeat the sequence of figures.

United Kingdom

Humphrey, Walter. "How to Dance the Tango." *Ballroom Dancing Times* (London, 1911); reprinted in *Ballroom Dancing Times,* October 1990, 12–13.

1st Mvt.: Promenade (?) forward, slow steps both starting with right, sliding the feet for eight bars. (An illustration shows backing the woman, but that means the partners need to start on opposite feet.)

2nd Mvt.: On slow beats: back right, left, close right, forward left, repeat.

3rd Mvt.: Double slides to the right and left, *ad libitum.*

4th Mvt.: The man crosses left in front, points right side and front, repeats to opposite side. The woman steps opposite (sweeping scissors?).

5th Mvt.: Join right hands, "*valse*" (turn?) across partner, the man starts forward and turns right, the woman starts back and turns left.

6th Mvt.: Back the woman four steps, starting forward right. Point right forward, *corte* back right. Step back left and *corte* forward left. Woman opposite.

7th Mvt.: "Crab" step from the one-step repertoire.

8th Mvt.: Slow turning *molinete.*

Raymond, Paul. "The Argentine Tango." *Dance Journal* 4 (January 1912): 11–12.

El Paseo: Back the woman, the man starts right forward.

El Medio corte: Forward right, side left and close right, back left and hold.

El Corte: Back left, right, left (QQS); end with weight leaning back left.

El Paseo con golpe: Side left, cross right in front, side left, coupe right.

El Volteo: Cross left in front, uncross right, cross left in front, uncross right and point to the side, reverse.

Note: all turns are to be done to the left.

de Fouquières, André. "Le tango." *Dance Journal* 5 (March 1913): 10–11.

El Paseo: Back the woman, starting forward right, end with a *corte* back left.

El Medio corte/2nd Figure: Cross left in front, take four steps to the right side, face partner with a side-close. Cross right in front, four steps side left, face partner with a side-close. Two *chassés* right, two *chassés* left.

3rd Figure: Side (?) right, cross left in front, uncross and forward right, side left, cross right in front, uncross and back left, repeat (QQS, QQS?).

4th Figure: Side right, cross left, uncross and side right, slow drag close left.

5th Figure: *Chassé* forward right, balance, back left, balance.

6th Figure: *Rueda* crossing right over left.

7th Figure: Forward right and left, *chassé* right, *chassé* left.

8th Figure: *Chassé* right, cross left forward, *chassé* left (?), cross left forward.

M. Robert. "The Tango." *Dance Journal* 5 (March 1913): 4.

1st Figure: Back the woman, end with forward right, side left and close right, back right. (In this case, either there is a misprint, and the man is to step back left, or the close right is done without weight, leaving the right foot free to step back.)

2nd Figure: Cross right behind, side left (turning slightly left), back left and hold, (side left without weight?).

3rd Figure: The woman's step for the second Figure—cross left in front, side right (turning slightly left), forward right and hold.

4th Figure: Turn in a left-turn waltz.

5th Figure: Cross right in front, close left, place right at the back, cross left in front, close right to side, place left to the front.

6th Figure: Cross right in front, cross left in front (scissors?).

7th Figure: Promenade SSQQ (face partner and *chassé* on quicks).

8th Figure: Partners walk and turn and pass in front of each other (Promenade?).

9th Figure: Small *chassés*, followed by a *rueda* in which the woman continues the *chassés*.

10th Figure: Box.

"The Argentine Tango." *Dance Journal* 5 (July 1913): 3–6.

El Paseo: Back the woman one step per bar.

La Marcha: Back the woman two steps per bar.

El Medio corte: Forward right, forward left and close right, back left and hold (SQQS and hold).

El Corte: Back right, side left and close right, back left and hold (SQQS and hold).

(Variations: *Cortes* can be done forward or backward—the man can do the woman's step and vice versa.)

El Rueda: The man crosses right over left, or left over right, or goes from one all the way around into the other.

Chester, S. Beach. *Secrets of the Tango.* London: T. Werner Laurie, 1914.

El Paseo: The man starts forward right, and takes five steps. Then he touches the left foot without weight beside the right, flicks the left toe forward slightly, and steps back left (SSSSSQQS).

El Corte: This is the finishing figure of *el paseo,* that is, touch/flick of the left foot and the step back with a pause. As the man does the touch/flick forward with his left foot, the woman does a touch/flick backward with her right foot (QQS).

Corte de la Dama: After *el corte,* the man can push the woman away, and she again does the touch/flick (alone this time). Then he steps back left and she steps forward right to complete another *corte.*

La Cruz: After a *corte,* the man crosses left in front, then right in front, and continues alternating crosses. The woman crosses right behind left, and also continues alternate crossings behind. When the man wishes to change the step, the couple does a little dip, and then reverses direction with the man crossing behind and the woman crossing in front.

Variation of La Cruz: The man crosses right front, the woman left behind. Continue crossing, end with a *corte.*

Corte de Lado: The man crosses right in front, turns left and steps forward in a new direction (or from ballroom position into promenade). Touch/flick backward left, forward left. Forward right, touch/flick and forward left. Three times total, end with *el paseo.*

Figura del Ebrio: The man crosses right in front, uncrosses the left, and steps side left, back right, and back left. The woman steps opposite, crossing behind.

El Ocho Argentino: In promenade position, the man steps forward left, and with feet apart, pivots toward his partner, flicking his left heel as he turns. The woman steps opposite. The couple is now in over-the-shoulders position. The man steps forward left (between himself and his partner), and forward right. He again pivots, flicking his right heel, and repeats the figure several times. The woman steps opposite. There are several misprints in the description of this step, but the diagrams concur with the interpretation given here.

La Rueda: The man crosses his right foot behind the left, and then his left foot behind the right. The woman steps around him, turning him as she goes. At the end, he steps into a *corte.*

La Media Luna: The man does a touch/flick forward left and steps back left. He then brings the right back and slightly to the side, touching without weight. He touch/flicks the right back, and steps forward right. He steps forward left without weight beside the right, and repeats. The woman steps opposite.

La Figura Criolla: The man crosses his right foot in front of his left, then uncrosses the left and steps side left, keeping weight on both feet. Rising on his toes, he pivots his heels slightly to the right, turning slightly left. The woman steps opposite, also crossing in front.

D'Albert, Charles. *Encyclopedia and Technical Glossary of the Art of Dancing.* London: T. M. Middleton, c. 1914.

El Paseo: Slowly back the woman, one step per bar.

El Marcha: Back the woman, two steps per bar.

El Medio corte: Forward right, left, close right, back left, pause (SQQS).

El Corte: Same as a *medio corte,* but the man can also end stepping forward after a half or quarter turn and can continue a string of turning *medio cortes*—hence four *medio cortes* make a *corte* of eight bars.

El Chase: Promenade SQQS.

Media luna: Box step: The man starts forward right (QQS QQS).

El Cruzado (scissors): Crossing steps variously linked, with a note about irregular phrases ended with *cortes.*

El Abanico: Side-cross-side and turn. Repeat on opposite foot.

El Rueda: The man crosses either right over left or left over right. The woman *chassés* around him.

La Vigne: Scissors step—the man goes forward, the woman backward. End with a *medio corte.*

El Ocho Argentino: In ballroom position, cross right in front, uncross left to the side back right, cross left in front uncross right to the side, forward left.

Repeat. Can be combined with *cruzados.* Rhythm?

El Frottado: Promenade forward right, sweep forward left, close right, back left, sweep right back, close left as she swings around to face; end with *medio corte.*

El Molinette: In skaters' or Yale position (D'Albert says side by side?). Forward left, right, left, close right, then back, alternate left and right, doing a one-eighth turn each step.

Richardson, P. J. S., ed. *The Guide to the Tango.* London: Francis, Day and Hunter, c. 1914.

Uriel Simmons and M. Robert

La Marche: Starting forward right, back the woman four steps.

Le Corte: Forward right, side left, close right, back left, hold.

Le Ciseaux: Cross right in front, walk four steps, turn on count four, cross left in front, walk four, turn on count four. Or, a half-time version: cross, turn, cross, turn.

La Media luna: Box (QQS QQS).

La Promenade: Starting forward right (QQSS, pause).

Alice Van Dyke

Paseo: Walk four steps.

Corte: Forward right, side left and close right, back left.

El Ocho: Starting left, side-cross-side, reverse.

Media luna: Box.

El Paseo del lado: Side left, cross right in front, side left, close right, repeat or reverse.

Las Tijeras: Side left, cross right, side left, cross right, touch left to the side, reverse.

Volteo: Grapevine.

M. *Givre*

El Paseo: Slow walk, one step per bar.

La Marcha: Walk with one step per beat (Two per bar).

El Corte: Forward right, left, cut right under, back left, hold.

El Medio corte: Back right, touch left to the side, pivot slightly, back left.

La Media luna: Corte forward and backward.

Paseo con golpe: Cross right, left in front, cut right under left, touch side left, strike heel. Repeat three times and end with a *corte.*

El Ocho: March with each dancer alternately passing in front of his partner (walk, walk, pivot, pivot?).

Las Tijeras: Cross right, three steps left, pivot, reverse.

La Rueda: Cross right over left, the woman walks around the man, end with a *corte.*

R. *De Alvez*

El Paseo: Forward right in a slow walk, can reverse.

El Corte: Forward right, left, stamp right, close left behind, back right.

El Cruzado: Forward right, sweep left forward and backward.

Corte con quebrado: Promenade position. Cross each foot in front of the other in alternation.

El Golpeado: During the *Paseo,* stamp right, step side right, stamp left.

La Rueda: The man crosses either foot, the woman *chassés* around the man.

Cruzado con corte: Cross right in front, uncross left, close right with a tap, reverse.

La Media luna: Two sweeping long steps forward, two back.

Walter Humphrey

El Paseo: Walk forward, starting right, step side left on count eight, leaving right extended to the side.

La Corte: Forward right, forward left, back right, back left, forward right with weight.

Media luna: Sweep right forward, sweep left forward, close right, sweep left back, sweep right back, close left.

Scissors: Cross right in front, side left, cross right, uncross left and point to the side, reverse. Then cross, point, cross, point, then four crosses.

Le Corte: Forward right, touch left forward, back left.

Half time step: Slow walk forward four steps, then four quick steps backward, then two slow forward.

Open Walk: Slow forward and backward walk, extending trailing leg behind. End with side left and point side right.

Tap step: Walk forward on counts one through four. Turn into promenade on five and six. Beat right heel forward and at the side of left heel on seven and eight.

Le Ronde: Cross behind, uncross, close, point, reverse. The woman crosses opposite.

Circa: Rueda. Cross right over left, the woman *chassés* around.

Eight Crosses: Cross right in front, uncross left, cross right in front (QQS), cross left in front, uncross right, cross left in front (same rhythm).

The Fan: Cross right in front, uncross left, cross right in front, side left and twist so partners' knees touch, trail left leg behind. Reverse.

Tango: Forward right, left, close right (QQS), back left and swing one-half left (?). Point right heel forward.

Little Tango: Shift weight from right to left and *coupe* right under left (QQS). Shift weight to right and extend left behind. Repeat three times, last time shifting weight back on left. Reverse.

Le Carne: Cross right, uncross left, cross right, side left plus one-quarter turn, four times to make a square.

Swepstone, Eileen. *How to Dance the Tango.* Vancouver, B.C.: J. H. Welch, 1914.

Tango One

Tango Walk: In promenade position, the woman walks six steps forward, turning a half turn on count six, and continuing two more steps in line of direction on the inside of the circle. The man walks two steps forward. On the third step, he turns in front of the woman, and walks backward on counts four and five (on the outside of the circle). On count six, the couple turns with the man walking forward (the couple walk forward around each other as in a Pomander turn) and turning into his original position, and the woman walking forward and pivoting slightly to resume promenade position.

Drag and Pivot: With the man facing out and the woman facing in, each steps to the side (toward line of direction) with their first feet, and drags the second feet to close. Repeat on counts three and four. End with four pivots.

Grape Vine with Dip: Alternating grapevine. Count seven, bend the second knee, pointing the first foot in line of direction. Count eight, close first foot to second.

Half Grape Vine, Dip, and Pivot: Backing the woman, the man takes one step forward right, and then steps forward left, crossing in front of the right. Bend the right knee, extending the left foot to the side. On count four, straighten the knee and close the feet together.

Tango Two

Position and Two-Step: Backing the woman, each dancer takes one small step in line of direction. On count two, point the second foot to the side, looking over the shoulders at the pointed foot. On counts three and four, do one two-step in line of direction. Repeat.

Dip, Two-Step, Walk, and Circle Foot: In promenade position, step forward on the first foot, dip forward bending the leading knee. Two-step forward on the inner foot, walk forward two steps (first foot, second foot), swing first (outside) foot in a *media luna* to meet partner's foot toes pointed to the floor.

Double Scissors: The man starting left, and the woman right, both do crossing scissors with points: cross first foot, cross second, cross first, point second to the side. Cross second, cross first, cross second, point first to the side. Does not give partners' positions relative to each other, but scissors are generally done with partners facing each other.

Tango Three

Reverse Walk: Four steps forward in promenade position, then flips on count five, and finishing with three more steps backing in right shoulder Yale position.

Dip and Turn: Facing partner (?), the man places left foot forward without weight (the woman back right), bending the other knee (two counts). Rise and pivot on three, four, and five. Opposite feet and knees for six and seven, ending with feet together on eight.

Dip and Two-Step: Same as the "Dip, Two-Step, Walk, and Circle Foot" in Tango Two.

Lady Pirouettes, Gentleman Walks: A *rueda,* except that the woman crosses left over right and the man walks around.

Tango Four

Sway and Balance: Sway from side to side, raising trailing foot off the floor, giving four counts to each side.

Sway Turning: Sway from side to side as in "Sway and Balance," but giving only two counts to each side and slowly making a complete turning eight counts.

Walk & Swing: Backing the woman, take three steps starting forward left. On count four, point right foot forward. On counts five through seven, swing right foot back, forward, back. On count eight, change weight to the right foot. (The woman steps opposite.)

The "Walk & Swing" is repeated as the fourth step of this tango. This step appears in one-step descriptions as the Castle Rock.

The Tango Two-Step

1. Partners hold hands in open position (the woman on the man's right side). Couple walks forward two steps, each starting on his own first foot, then close the feet on count three, bend and pivot slightly away from partner. Repeat on opposite feet, facing partner (four, five, and six). On seven and eight, she steps around to ballroom position.

2. Dip and Two-Step as in Tango Two, number two, repeat.

3. Four two steps: backing the woman, turning backing the man (turning?).

4. Backing the man, the woman dips forward on her right knee, and the man dips back left. Then one two-step forward Repeat. Then do thirty-two bars of "ordinary" (turning?) two-step.

(Note: Of all the tango sources surveyed here, Swepstone's is the only one to favor the woman backing the man and to give the steps from the woman's point of view.)

France

Robert, L. *Théorie du vrai tango argentin.* Paris: Salabert, c. 1911 (sheet music).

1st Figure: Back the woman with a forward, side-close, back, hold *corte.*

2nd Figure: Cross right behind left, point left to the left, turn slowly, bend left, point right.

3rd Figure: Reverse 2nd Figure. One partner does 2nd Figure while the other does 3rd Figure.

4th Figure: Left turn waltz ending with Figures 2/3.

5th Figure: *Ocho.* Cross right, uncross left, cross left, uncross right.

6th Figure: Typical scissors step.

7th Figure: Side right, forward left and close right, repeat to the other side.

8th Figure: *"Petite Marche."* Obscure: the man passes the woman in front of him.

9th Figure: *Rueda.*

10th Figure: *Pas Carré* (Box).

Professor Bacton. *Théorie complète et authentique du tango argentin.* [Paris]: n.p., 1912 (sheet music).

El Paseo: Forward right, backing the woman one step per bar.

La Marcha: Back the woman two steps per bar.

Medio corte: Forward right, side left and close right, back left and hold (SQQS and hold).

El corte: Cross right behind, side left, close right, back left and slowly *plié* back on left (SQQS-*plié* and hold).

La Media luna: Box.

El Cruzado: Cross right behind, side left, cross right behind, point left side, repeat to the other side.

El Chase: Side left, cross right behind, side left, close right in air (?) with half waltz turn, repeat, starting on the other leg.

Ocho Argentino: Cross right behind, side left, back right, cross left behind, side right, forward left.

La Rueda: Cross left over right, the woman *glissades* around the man.

El Frottado: Forward left using "polishing" motion.

El Abanico: Side left, cross right behind, back left, pass behind the woman, reverse.

El Molinete: Cross left, right behind, cross left behind right, pivot on toe of left, put right behind, pivot on right heel, pivot on left toe, right heel, keep turning.

Minchin, Madame. *Théorie du tango argentin.* Paris: Durand, 1912 (pamphlet)

Paseo: Back the woman, man starts forward right.

Corte: Stop on right, step side left, close right (SQQ), then back left and hold (SS). Repeat.

El Ocho: Ballroom position. The man crosses right in front, the woman crosses left behind. Cross, join the other foot to the stepped foot, pivot.

Media luna: Box step, with the man starting forward right.

El Paseo del lado: Side-cross-side, box.

Las Tijeras: Side-cross-side-cross-point, reverse.

Volteo: Grapevine alternating crosses in front and behind.

Rivera, Max. *Les tango et les dances nouvelles.* Paris: Pierre LaFitte, 1913.

1st Fig.: Five steps forward, starting right; close left and part heels, back left and pause.

2nd Fig.: Cross left in front, four steps to the right, ending with a *chassé* freeing the right, cross right in front and repeat. Do twice to each side. Then cut in half and do *chassés* right, left, right, left. The woman steps opposite, also crosses front.

3rd Fig.: Cross left in front, side right, slightly ahead, forward and left with left, cross right over left, side left slightly behind, repeat, end with *chassé* left.

4th Fig.: Promenade (?) SSQQ(S?), *chassé* on quicks, alternate direction (?).

La Media luna: Cortes (1st Fig.) forward left and back right.

6th Fig.: *Rueda,* crossing right over left.

7th Fig.: Forward left, right (SS), *chassé* forward and back (QS?), repeat.

8th Fig.: Two-step (polka without a hop), backing the woman, turning (twisting?).

9th Fig.: Back the woman four slow steps, starting forward left. Balance forward and back, touching left even with right and stepping back left.

10th Fig.: Unintelligible!

Bayo and Chrysis. *Le Tango Argentin.* [Paris]: n.p., c. 1914 (sheet music).

First Fig.: Back the woman four steps, bring left back, pause.

Second Fig.: Cross left front, uncross right, cross left front, uncross right (without weight), cross right front, uncross left, cross right front, uncross left.

Repeat, then four crosses in front. The woman steps on opposite feet, but also crosses front.

Third Fig.: (Skaters' *Ocho*), Forward right, cross left in front, uncross right, forward left, cross right, uncross left, repeat, ending with *chassé* left.

Fourth Fig.: Promenade two slow steps, face partner for a QQ side-close (this pattern three times), reverse, reverse and repeat, end with four QQS *chassés* (48 counts).

Media luna: Corte forward left, back right; woman opposite.

Sixth Fig.: *Rueda,* crossing left over right, only a half turn.

Seventh Fig.: Back the woman two steps, *chassé* forward left, right. The woman steps opposite. Pause, repeat.

Eighth Fig.: *Chassé* forward right and left, keeping leading foot crossed in front. The woman keeps leading foot crossed behind (successive lock steps).

Les 15 danses modernes. France/Algiers: n.p., c. 1920s.

Pas Argentin: Forward right, back left, side right, close left.

Le Corte: Half-box *corte* in all possible directions; that is, forward (or back), side-close, back (or forward).

El Cruzado: Side right, cross left behind, slowly *glissé* right in front and forward, pivot left. Repeat, starting left.

L'Eventail: Side left, cross right behind, *glissé* left to the left, shift weight onto the left, reverse.

Media luna: Forward right, sweep left back and forward, shift weight onto left, sweep right back and forward, close in front.

Media luna sur le côté: (Media luna to the side.)

Le Huit: Side right, cross left behind, side right, pivot right, side left, cross right behind, uncross left. (No rhythm given, but possibly QQS QQS, eliding the side right and pivot right into one motion.)

Les Ciseaux: Cross right behind, point left side, cross left behind, point right side, repeat.

Danses nouvelles. Paris: Albin Michel, 1920.

Marche: Back the woman (no rhythm or tempo given).

Corte sur place: Forward right, side left and close right, back left and hold (SQQS and hold).

Corte: Same as *corte sur place,* but the man starts back right.

Media luna: Box.

Promenade: Walk SQQS, then cross right, uncross left, close right, pause.

Huit: Forward right, side left, cross right, front, back left, side right, cross left front, repeat.

Petits ciseaux: Cross right front, side left, close right, cross left front, side right, close left (SQQ SQQ).

Pas du crabe: Side left, cross right front, side left, back right.

Vade mecum du parfait danseur–Les danses en vogue. Paris: F. D. Marchetti, 1920.

1: Back the woman two steps per bar, ending with *corte.*

2: Two more *cortes,* right and left.

3: Scissors: side-cross-side-point, reverse.

4: Front cross steps.

5: Forward left, close right without weight, forward right, close left without weight, repeat.

6: Four *glissés* (side-close) left, four *glisses* right.

7: Four cross steps left to turn in a left circle, repeat right.

8: Two *glissés* behind left-close-right, pivot to face right. Repeat forward right, always turning right.

1 Figure: Forward left-close right-left, back right. Repeat to the right. (Although the author does not specify it, it seems necessary to shift the weight onto the left foot in order to step out again onto the right.)

2 Figure: In promenade position. Forward left, close right behind, pivot, repeat forward right.

3 Figure: *Paseo.* Forward left, right, left, close right behind.

4 Figure: *Rueda.*

5 Figure: *Media luna.* Forward right, sweep left forward, close right, sweep left, right behind, close left.

6 Figure: *Le Volteo.* A typical grapevine.

Charles, D. *Toutes les danses modernes et leurs théories complètes.* Paris: S. Bornemann, c. 1920s (pp. 45–57).

Marche: Slow walk, backing the woman, taking one step per (slow) beat of music.

Marche battue: Back the woman, taking two steps per slow beat of music. The man starts forward right.

Marche Argentine avant: Forward right, forward left, side right, close left to right, pause (SQQS).

Marche Argentine arrière: Back left, back right, side left, close right to left, pause (SQQS).

Promenade Argentine: Facing partner, step side left, cross right in front, uncross left to the left side, close right to left (SQQS).

Promenade Argentine battue: Side left, stamp right close to the left, cross right front, uncross left to the side, *glissé* the right closer to the left, stamp left close to right (QQQQQQ).

Promenade Argentine battue retirée: "The first three half-beats (Qs) as in the preceding step." Then close the left to the right, slowly step back on the right, and pause (QQQQS).

Promenade Argentine échappée: Side left, cross right in front, uncross left to the left side, close right to left, step forward left, close right to left (SQQSQQ?).

Promenade Argentine double échappée: To the preceding figure, add another step forward left, and close right to left.

Promenade Argentine (variante): Side left, close right to left, side left, cross right in front, uncross left to the left side, close right to left (QQS QQS?).

Promenade Argentine tournée: Side left, cross right in front, uncross left to the side, close right to left. During these four steps, make a half turn to the right. Finish by stepping forward left (the illustration shows the forward left to be a *corte*).

Promenade Argentine (variante): Side left, cross right in front, uncross left to the left side, again cross right in front, pause (SQQS).

Promenade Argentine (variante): After completing the above step, un-cross the left to the left side, and cross the right tightly behind the left (SQQ SQQ?). The woman also crosses behind at the end.

Promenade Argentine (variante): Side left, cross right in front, without uncrossing slide the left closer to the right, close the right tightly to the left, uncross the left and bring it to the side of the right, slowly step back right (SQQQQS?)

Pour terminer une Promenade Argentine: Side left, cross the right tightly in front of the left, pivot a quarter turn left, step forward left, side right, and close left to right (SQQ SQQ).

Pas battu de côté: Side left, cross right in front, uncross left and step forward, side right, stamp left close to right (SQQS).

Autre pas battu pour passer de la position arrière à celle de côté: Step back left, then back right. Step forward left, turning one quarter to the left. Sweep right to the side. Close left to right. Rhythm is SQQQQ.

Grand Assemblé: Step forward right, close left to right, step back slightly with right and pause (QQS). Repeat, starting forward left.

Grand Assemblé croisé: Step forward right; bring the left forward until it is crossed behind the right. Pull the right back until it is closed tightly to the left, pause (QQS). Repeat, starting forward left.

Marche Assemblée: Step forward right, forward left, cross the right be-hind the left, pause (QQS).

Croisé Américain: Begin with a small step side right. Stamp left close to right. Step side left, cross right in front and ahead, uncross left, step forward (QQSSS). The woman steps side left and stamps right close to left. Then side right, back left, right.

Pas en spirale simple demi-tour: Step forward left, forward right. Rise on toes and do a half turn left. End with the feet closed tightly to-gether with the left crossed in front, pause. Step back right, side left, close the right to the left (QQS QQS).

Pas en spirale simple 3/4 de tour: Step forward left, right. Rise onto toes and turn one-half left. End with the feet closed tightly together, left crossed in front, pause. Step back right, turning one more quar-ter left. Step side left, close right to left (QQS QQS).

Pas en spirale simple tour complet: Step forward left, right. Rise onto toes and do a half turn left. End with the feet closed tightly together, left crossed in front, pause. Step back, right, turning one more quarter left. Step side left, turning the last quarter left to complete the second half-turn. Step side right, close left to right (QQS QQQQ).

Pas en spirale double tour complet: Step forward left, right. Rise onto toes and do a half turn left. End with the feet closed tightly together, left crossed in front, pause. Step back right, left. Rise onto toes and do another half turn left. End with the feet closed tightly together, left crossed in front, pause. Step forward left, side right. Close the left to the right, pause (QQS QQS QQS).

Pas en spirale, double tour complet, croisements inversés: Same as above, but as the turns are made the left leg swings out and crosses behind the right.

Spirale coupée: Step forward left, right, pivot one-half left on the right foot only, ending with left crossed in front (not tightly), pause. Uncross right, step side right, continuing one-quarter left turn. Step back left, right, again turn one-quarter left (now facing the original direction). Bring left foot back to cross tightly in front of the right (QQS QQQQ).

Spirale décroisée: Step forward left turning slightly left. Step forward right, continuing slight turn left, Step forward left, finishing a half turn, pause. Step back right, turning slightly left. Step back left. Continuing slight turn left. Step back right to complete the second half turn, pause (QQS QQS).

Le tour en spirale: Step side left with the left. Cross the right in front. Pivot one quarter turn left and close the feet side by side. Slowly move the right slightly back, pause. To finish the half turn, step forward left and turn one quarter to the left, step back right and left continuing to turn to the left, bring right slowly back (SQQS SQQS).

Spirale Habanera: Step forward left, forward right. Pivot one-half around, ending with left crossed in front of right. Uncross right and step side right. Step forward left, making another quarter turn to the left. Slight step side right, keeping feet apart. Slight step side left, turning slightly left, keeping feet apart. Step forward right (all the way ahead of left), completing the last quarter turn, step forward left (QQS SQQSSS?).

Pas de fantaisie: Step side left, turning left. Continuing to turn, cross right in front of left. Rising onto the toes, pivot one-half turn left. Step back right, pause. Step forward left without weight, *glissé* the left to the right side, close right forward by left. Repeat one time forward (?). Step side right with the right, close left to right (SQQS QQQQS?).

Pas de fantasie (variante): Step forward diagonally left with the left foot; continue making a quarter turn left by taking two more steps. Step back right, left, right, cross the left in front, then cross the right in front, pause (QQQQQQQS).

Peters, A. *Le tango: Les nouveaux pas du tango.* Paris: Editions Nilsson, c. 1920s.

Le Tango

La Marcha: Back the woman, walking two steps per measure.

La Marcha (en Arrière): Back the man, two steps per measure.

El Medio corte (en Arrière): The man steps forward right, side left and close right, back left and hold (SQQS). The woman opposite.

(en Avant): The man steps back left, side right, and close left, forward right and hold (SQQS). The woman steps opposite.

El Corte (en Arrière): The man steps back right, side left and close right, back left and hold (SQQS). The woman steps opposite.

(en Avant): The man steps forward left, side right and close left, forward right and hold (SQQS).

Demi-tour du Pied Droit: The man steps back right, places left behind right and pivots left (QQ), then closes right beside left on count two.

Demi-tour du Pied Gauche: The man steps forward left, places right ahead of left and pivots left (QQ), then completes the turn by stepping back right and closing left to the side of right.

La Media luna (du Pied Droit): The man steps forward right, side left, and closes right (QQS).

(du Pied Gauche): The man steps back left, side right, and closes left (QQS).

El Chase (à Gauche): The man steps side left, crosses right in front, un-crosses left to the side, closes right (SQQS). Left foot points in line of direction, right foot is at a right angle to the left.

(à Droit): Side right, cross left front, uncross right side and close left (SQQS). Right foot points in line of direction, left is at a right angle.

El Cruzado (à Gauche): The man crosses right in front to the side, un-crosses left beside right, and turns slightly to the right, pivoting heels to the left.

(à Droit): The man crosses left in front to the side, uncrosses right be-side left, and turns slightly to the left, pivoting heels to the right.

Illustrations for both *cruzados* show the woman stepping opposite.

La Rueda: The man crosses right over left, the woman steps around him crossing left over right, and uncrossing.

El Ocho Argentino: The man steps in place left, crosses right in front, uncrosses left to the side, backs right, crosses left front, uncrosses right behind (possible rhythm: SQQ SQQ). This *ocho* often appears in skaters' position, but here it is suggested that partners face each other, using opposite feet, with the woman starting halfway through the step (step right in place, cross left behind, uncross right to the side, forward left, cross right behind, uncross left in front).

El Abanico: The man steps side left, crosses right front, uncrosses left behind, pivots left as right sweeps around to the side (making a quarter turn right), crosses left front, uncrosses right behind (rhythm: SQQ SQQ?). The woman begins at the halfway point.

El Paseo (en Avant): Back the woman starting forward left. *Plié* on the "&" of one. Rise on two, bring the right foot slightly forward. Con-tinue, alternate feet. The woman steps opposite.

(en Arrière): Back the man, starting back right. *Plié* on the "&" of one. Rise on two, bring the left foot slightly back. Continue, alternate feet. The woman steps opposite.

El Frotado (à Gauche): The man steps forward right, then forward diag-onally left. Close right to left, then back diagonally with the left. Close right to left, then step forward diagonally left. Continue through the "&" of count five, close right on six (S), step back left on count seven and hold (S).

(à Droit): Reverse the direction of the above.

El Molinete: The man crosses left foot in front of right, then right foot in front of left. Then step forward left, turning one quarter left. The shift the weight back onto the right heel, turning one quarter left. Then shift forward onto the left toes, turning one quarter. Continue through the end of the phrase. The woman crosses opposite feet and direction.

Les Nouveaux Pas du Tango

March Argentine (en Avant): Backing the woman, the man steps forward right, left, and then closes right to left (QQS). The woman steps opposite.

(en Arrière): Backing the man, the woman steps forward right, left, closes right to left (QQS). The man steps opposite.

Enchaînements: Backing the woman, the man steps forward right, left, side right, and closes left to right. Continue by again stepping forward right. The rhythm is SSQQ. The woman steps opposite.

Pas de Dentelle: Same as *Enchaînements,* except the man steps backward (starting left), and the woman forward.

Pas de Dentelle sans Tourner: A grapevine that alternates crosses in front and behind, twisting the body to the left when crossing in front, and to the right when crossing behind. The woman steps opposite.

Pas de Dentelle en Tournant: The man steps side left and crosses right front. Then uncrosses the left behind, pivoting slightly right until the left is directly behind the right. Then he sweeps left in front, pivoting another quarter turn right. He steps forward left, right, pivots slightly right as he sweeps the right behind. To finish, he sweeps the left in front, and completes the pivot to the right.

Temps d'Arrêt: The man steps back right, left, turning one quarter left. With another quarter turn left, he steps side right and closes left (SSQQ). The woman steps forward left, right, also turning one quarter left, then completing the left turn, she steps side left and closes right to left.

Balancé: The man steps forward (or back) on either foot, with weight. He then shifts weight onto the original foot. Balances can be done with either foot, and chained together. The woman steps opposite.

Le Pas Marqué (en Avant): A slow walk backing the woman, placing all the weight on the foot that is forward.

(en Arrière): A slow walk backing the man, placing the weight entirely on the stepping foot. Peters suggests chaining the two *pas marque* steps together with the balance steps.

Germany

Koebner, F. W. *Tanz Brevier.* Berlin: Verlag Dr. Eysler, 1913.

Promenade: Back the woman four steps, touch left forward and step back left.

Scissors: The woman *chassés* back and forth in front of the man as he supports her.

Rueda: The man crosses one foot over the other, the woman travels around him.

Promenade 2: Forward left, right, left, cross right and uncross left, turning to repeat in opposite direction.

Steinke, A., with Willi Weissbart. *Tango Galiziano.* Berlin: Orpheus-Verlag, c. 1914 (sheet music).

1st Figure: Back the woman left, right, left, right, close left without weight, back left.

2nd Figure: Touch left side and draw closed, bend right knee, reverse.

3rd Figure: Touch right side, close with weight, three waltz steps turning right, reverse.

4th Figure: Slow (Argentine) waltz.

5th Figure: Promenade position: left, right, left, dip left knee, turn outward, repeat in reverse.

6th Figure: Promenade position: Scissors. Both partners do scissors toward each other starting on their own first feet, then the woman continues on alone.

7th Figure: Back the woman, both cross-stepping, then half turn; continue, backing the man.

8th Figure: Deep dips at significant places in the rhythm.

9th Figure: Vague. Turn the woman under the man's raised left arm?

Bergen, Rolfe. *Der Tanz.* Munich: Druck der Innsbrucker Buchdruckerei und Verlagsanstalt, 1915.

Introduction and *corte:* Back the woman, end with forward right, touch left to right, back left.

[Cross]: Alternate *cortes,* turning to form a cross.

Scissors: Step across with second foot, pivot and pause, step across with first foot, pivot and pause, etc.

Media-luna: Tango step forward and back, and sweep on the backward steps.

Lady's Cross-Step: Typical *rueda:* ends with the woman doing a back step, then both *corte.*

Great Cross-Step: Grapevine, with turning.

Italy and Spain

Pichetti, E. *La danza antica e moderna.* Rome: n.p., 1914.

Paseo: Back the woman four slow steps, starting forward right.

Medio corte: Forward right, side left and close right, back left (SQQS).

Medio luna: Box plus *medio corte.*

El Chase: Cross right over left, uncross and *chassé, chassé* three more times, then *medio corte.*

Corte: Back right, side left and close right, back left, repeat.

Valise: Back right, forward left, finish with a *corte.*

Cruzado: Cross right in front, uncross left, cross right in front, then a quick left-right *chassé.* Repeat to the right side. *Chassé* left and right (QQS QQS), end with a *medio corte.*

5th Figure: Cross right, uncross left and chase (SQQS), repeat. Cross right over left as the woman does a six step *rueda,* end with a *medio corte.*

Rueda a destra: Reverse of 5th Figure.

El Ocho: Alternating traveling *ochos* with ones in place, each partner does the opposite, end with *medio corte.*

Open *media luna:* Promenade position. Forward right, left, the woman steps in front for repeated forward right, back left (rocking?) *media luna.*

El Zapateo: Side right, close left, *chassé* forward right, *chassés* back right, repeat twice, finish with *medio corte.*

10th Figure: Four twisting *chassés,* starting cross right (QQS). Then four slow scissors, starting cross right in front. End with *medio corte.* The woman starts *chassés* crossing left behind.

Stell y Pelicer, Condessa. "Tango argentino." In *Danzas Modernas.* Madrid: Antonio Izquierdo, 1915.

Corte: Back the woman four steps starting forward right, close right without weight, side right and close left, forward right, left, close right without weight, side right and close left, forward right and left, close right without weight, back right and pause. (Possibly SSSS SQQ SS SQQ SSSS pause.)

Figure 2: Cross left in front and, turning to the right, walk five steps, reverse two counts, walk four steps, turn back to line of direction on count twelve. Cross left in front, point right side, cross right in front, point left side (seven counts), end crossing right over left, begin *rueda,* and end facing partner. The woman steps opposite, then walks around the man in the *rueda.*

Figure 3: Cross right over left, turning left, then side left, point, face partner and close left on count three. Repeat *ad libitum.*

Figure 4: Box, beginning forward right. On last close left, touch without weight. Then six steps forward, always closing right even with left. Cross left behind, side right and close left without weight. Touch left back and forward.

Figure 5: Unintelligible!

Figure 6: Right foot crab step alternating heel and toe, then left foot zigzags forward and back. Woman opposite.

Appendix 2. A Sampling of *New York Times* Article Titles on the Tango, 1911, 1913, and 1914

All the new dances (one-step, maxixe, foxtrot, and the animal dances, or "trots") were often in the newspaper headlines, as even a quick glance at the *New York Times* indexes for the first years after the tango arrived in the Northern Hemisphere shows. The tango and the turkey trot were the ones most frequently written about. It is interesting to note that both acceptance and condemnation of the new dances, particularly the tango, cut across cultural, economic, social, civic, and ecclesiastic strata.

1911

"Paris Has New Dance Called Argentine Largo Inspired by US Negroes," January 15, pt. 3, 3:4

"New Dance Long Boston Called Turkey Trot in Coney Island," January 29, pt. 5, 9:4

"Some Steps of New Dance Called the Tango Illustrated," February 19, pt. 7, 9

"Dance Hall Regulations," March 1, 2:4, March 2, 7:5, March 3, 3:6, March 10, 7:2, June 13, 1:6

"NYC Dance Masters Back Resolution Requiring Bonding," May 17, 8:4

"Sultzer's Dance Hall, Coney Island, Ejects Two US Soldiers" [for tangoing in uniform], July 27, 1:1

"NYC Aldermen Adopt Resolution Banning Certain Kinds of Public Dances That Endanger Girls' Morals," September 20, 3:4

"Berlin Police Suppress New Dance Apache, Also Called Schiebe, as Dangerous and Improper," October 15, pt. 4, 2:7

"M. Maurice, Who Learned to Dance in Paris, Has Now Returned to Introduce New Dances into NY Society," December 10, pt. 6, 10

"Philadelphia Society Leaders Approve Turkey Trot," December 22, 13:4

"M. Maurice Questions Prudishness of Parisians," December 24, pt. 4, 11:5

1913

"NYC Committee on Amusement Resources of Working Girls Approves Certain Modern Dances," February 8, 13:3

Between April and June the mayor wrote a series of articles in which he gave his opinions on dance halls, tea dances, and regulations for them.

"'Tea Dances'—Rev. W. T. Sumner Expresses His Disapproval," April 10, 6:4

"London Peeress Shocked at Modern Dances," May 20, 4:4

"Peeress's Letter Discussed in London," May 21, 3:4

"Turkey Trot Banned at Panama," May 21, 3:4

"Tango to Be Introduced at Tea Dances in London," May 23, 3:6

"Paris—Mlle. Villany Fined," May 25, pt. 3, 5:3

"Freak Dances Denounced by Father Vaughan in London," May 26, 3:6

"Turkey Trotting in NYC Hotels Condemned by Grand Jury in Presentment," May 28, 7:4

"Mayor Gaynor Resents Presentment," May 29, 6:4

"Extract from Lady Middleton's Letter," June 3, 3:7

"Lenox, Mass. Censor Resigns," June 16, 3:5

"Tango Party Given by Mrs. John Astor in London, None Given by the Duchess of Marlborough," June 17, 4:2

Editorial: "Objectionable Names of New Dances," June 18, 8:2

"Donald D. Bartholomew Ejected from Orange High School Dance for Turkey Trotting," June 25, 1:2

"Swiss Hotels Prohibit 'American' Dances—Austrian Officer Challenges Daughter's American Partner to Duel," July 10, 3:7

"Turkey Trot—Prussian Officer Killed by General in Duel over Its Propriety," July 26, 1:7

Editorial on Prussian officer's death, August 1, 6:5

"London Press Discussion and Letter by Lady Middleton," special article, August 24, pt. 5, 5:1

"Paris Turns to the Quadrille in Place of the Tango," August 24

"Modern Dances Condemned by Canon Newbolt in London," August 25, 3:7

Editorial on Canon Newbolt, August 26, 8:3

"Government Control of Tango Advised by Princess Lowenstein Wertheimer," September 14, pt. 2, 1:7

"Tango Defended by Jean Richepin," September 21, pt. 3, 1:1

"Duke d'Abruzzi Blamed for Corrupting Italian Society by the Tango," October 4, 4:4

"Nutley, New Jersey, Submits Question of the Tango to a Referendum Vote," October 6, 2:6

Germany—"Tango Popular on Stage," October 6, 3:5

"Tango Teas in Stores," October 19, pt. 3, 2:2

"Society Girls Give Lessons, Demand Music," November 9, pt. 2, 3:3

"German Emperor Forbids Army and Navy Officers to Dance Tango, One-Step, or Two-Step in Uniform, Royal Opera Ballet Warned," November 18, 4:1

"Formal Order Denied, but Disapproval Expressed," November 19, 3:4

"Decree Ineffectual," November 23, pt. 4, 2:7

"Tango Banned at American Thanksgiving Celebration until Official Guests Leave," November 30, pt. 3, 4:4

"Kaiser Banned Tango Because Crown Princess Was Learning It," December 2, 4:5

"London Society Forms Tango Clubs," October 8, 8:4

"Tango Forbidden in Boston Public Dance Halls," October 12, pt. 3, 1:2

Cleveland—"Tango Barred, Asa Anderson Starts Suit, Exhibits Tango for Judge Vickery," October 16, 1:7

"Chicago City Council Will Investigate the Tango," October 17, 1:7

"French Academy Hears Lecture on the Tango by Jean Richepin," October 26, pt. 3, 4:6 (text reprinted November 16, pt. 7, 12:1)

"Comment on Tango from London Club Man," November 2, pt. 3, 2:3

"Vatican to Leave Decision on the Tango to the Bishops," November 2, pt. 3, 2:3

"Origin Not Classic, Richepin's Statement Questioned," November 9, pt. 3, 3:3

"NYC Restaurants Cater to Craze for Modern Dances," November 13, 20:3

"Tango Craze," November 16, pt. 3, 3:1

"Tango Prohibited by the Vatican," November 21, 1:5

"Bavarian King Puts Ban on Tango; Does Not Wish Army Officers to Be at Events Where It Is Danced," December 16, 3:6

"Attempt to Suppress Tango Fails," December 27, 1:7

"Minuet May Take Place of Tango in London," December 28, pt. 3, 4:2

"Italian King Forbids the Tango at State Ball," December 30, 4:5

1914

"Roman Catholic Church Clergy in NYC Fight the Tango," January 2, 9:3

"Tango Defended by Reverend D. S. Phelan of St. Louis, MO," January 4, pt. 2, 13:4

"Tango Discussed by Society Leaders in Paris," January 4, pt. 3, 3:3

"Tango Discussed by London Society Leaders," January 4, pt. 3, 3:3

Special article on the prevalence of the tango, January 4, pt. 5, 8:1

"Preachers Approve Ban on the Tango, Opinions of Others," January 5, 5:1

"Selected Gathering Votes That Tango Is Not Immodest," January 6, 4:5

Editorial putting the blame on the dancers, January 6, 12:3

"Ecclesiastical Authorities Denounce the Tango, Cardinal May Issue Decree," January 7, 4:3

Tango defended in letters by Uriel Davis, Vernon Castle, and H. M. Patterson, January 7, 10:6

Reply to Vernon Castle by Rev. Edward Mack, January 9, 10:6

"White Plains, NY—Ban on Tango May Stop Military Ball," January 9, 20:3

"Cardinal Bans Tango," January 10, 4:5

"Swiss Police Expel Teachers from Dance hall, Society Applauds Tango," January 12, 3:4

"Berlin Police Forbid 'Offensive Dances' in Public," January 12, 3:4

"Paris Academy of Dancing Masters Announces 'Tatao,' Chinese Dance, to Supplant Tango," January 15, 1:5

"Rev. Phelan Reproved by Archbishop Glennon for Tango Editorials," January 17, 1:8

"Aristocracy of Rome Accepts Prohibition, Archbishop of Florence Joins in Condemnation of Tango," January 17, 2:8

"Dance Continues in Spite of Ban," January 18, pt. 3, 2:7

"Academy Will Attempt to Codify the Tango, International Congress of Dancing Masters to Be Called," January 18, pt. 3, 2:7

"Eight Bishops in Provinces Ban the Tango," January 19, 2:1

"M. Stilson to Sue Cardinal Arnette for $20,000 Damages, Says Ban Has Caused Him to Lose Pupils," January 21, 4:5

"Cardinal Cavallari of Venice Issues Episcopal Letter, Severe Penances Established in Rome for Catholics Not Complying with Order," January 22, 4:5

"St. Paul's Episcopal Church, Patchogue, Long Island, to Give Exhibition of Proper Way to Dance the Tango," January 23, 7:8

"Seven More Bishops Prohibit the Tango," January 25, pt. 3, 2:8

"Tango Praised by Rabbi Jacob Nieto," January 26, 7:2

"Tango Introduced [in Japan] by John L. Mott and Mrs. Browne," January 26, 7:2

"Pope Sees the Tango, Causes the Venetian Furlana to Be Taught to Dancers Who Visited Him," January 28, 4:3

"Case to Be Heard," January 29, 4:3

"Exhibition of New Dances Given for NYC Board of Education," January 31, 6:3

"Furlana Becoming Popular," February 2, 3:2

"Comment of Dr. Welzmiller in Substituting Folk Dances for Tango at Y.M.C.A.," February 2, 5:3

"Atlantic City—Mrs. Lillian Boniface Albers Forced to Resign from Church Choir," February 3, 1:7

"Guests at Dances to Be Given by [French] President and Mme. Poincaré Will Be Asked Not to Dance the Tango," February 9, 3:2

"President Poincaré Bans the Tango at the Elysée," February 15, pt. 3, 2:2

Letter to the editor attributing cure of indigestion to new dances, February 18, 8:5

"Philippine Island Dances Compared by Dean C. Worcester with the Tango," February 21, 18:4

"Queen Alexandra and Mother Devoted to Tango," March 2, 1:2

"Philadelphia Tango Classes to Continue through Lent," March 9, 2:7

"Legislative Committee on Social Welfare Refuses to Accept Bill against the New Dances," March 14, 8:4

"Tango Thieves Active in Paris," March 15, pt. 4, 2:4

Gradually throughout 1914 the tango is singled out less often, and protests about and approvals of the new dances began to even out.

"Maxixe Considered Immoral in Brazil," April 10, 12:5

"Tango Defined by the Pope," April 12, pt. 3, 1:4

"Tango Called Injurious by Miss Lindley," April 26, pt. 8, 15:3

Letter by Dr. William G. Anderson on dancing as exercise from a psychological point of view, April 30, 10:7

"Kaiser Discusses Modern Dances with Mme. Pavlowa," May 17, pt. 3, 4:3

Special article by Owen Johnson on "Feminism and the Dance Craze," May 24, pt. 5, 6:1

"Hotels to Admit New Dances to Roof Gardens," May 31, pt. 2, 12:1

"New Dances Popular at Coney Island," May 31, pt. 3, 5:3

"Ritz-Carlton Not to Have Dancing on Roof Garden," June 1, 20:4

"Modern Dances Approved by Dancing Masters' Convention," June 13, 2:8

"Queen Mary Likes Tango Danced by Maurice and Partner," June 13, 3:1

"McAlpin and Astor Roof Gardens, Open, Many Dance at the Knicker-bocker and Waldorf," June 16, 6:2

"General Federation of Women's Clubs Denounces Immodest Dancing," June 16, 9:3

"Methodist Episcopal Sunday School at Nostrand Ave., Brooklyn, Disbanded on Account of Controversy over Hardwood Floor," June 30, 20:1

"Dancing Too Absorbing for Men and Women, Opinion of Mrs. S. Baruch," July 12, pt. 6, 4:1

"C. H. Taylor at London Congress of Imperial Society of Dancers Explains Why Tango Was Killed," July 28, 4:6

"Model Dance Hall on Strand Theatre to be Opened by Mrs. W. K. Vanderbilt, Miss Morgan and Others," December 17, 13:1

"Step toward Standardization Taken by Philadelphia Teachers," December 22, 1:2

Notes

Introduction

1. Savigliano, *Tango,* 241. Savigliano does not give a date for these documents; hence it may be that the following 1856 description is the earliest.

2. See chapter 5 for a discussion of the 1856 tango and its historical context, with a possible musical match.

3. See chapter 1 for a discussion of this theory.

4. According to José Gobello's *Diccionario Lunfardo,* 140–141, *mufarse* refers to a state of tedium, bad luck, ill-humor, soul-deep sadness, with a touch of ability to enjoy and wallow in one's own melancholy.

5. This accordion-like instrument came to symbolize the tango after 1900. See chapter 4 for a more complete description of its history and mechanics.

6. A multipurpose word that means both a dance form different from the tango and a gathering where the tango is danced socially.

7. Dr. Patri Pugliese, a Boston scholar who specializes in aspects of nineteenth-century social life, shares his collection of the major dance masters' works, including manuals by Wilson, Howe, Durang, Dodworth, the Castles, Mouvet, Clendenen, Walker, and many others. He also provides information on nineteenth-century games and pastimes, clothing styles, and resources for re-creating Victorian clothing patterns.

8. Faulkner, *Lure of the Dance.* Faulkner was a former member of the Los Angeles Dancing Academy and president of the Dancing Masters' Association of the Pacific Coast. He published a similar book in 1892 entitled *From the Ballroom to Hell,* its title borrowed by Elizabeth Aldrich for her summary of nineteenth-century social dance.

9. Von Bruch, *Carnival of Death,* 47.

1. The Origins of the Tango

1. See Gesualdo, *Historia,* 237–279, for descriptions of early musical life in Buenos Aires.

2. Gesualdo, *La musica,* 106–108.

3. In *La tribuna* (Buenos Aires) of July 1867 there was an advertisement for a tango on a motif "de la Yona" arranged for piano by M. D. de Antonan, available in the music shop of Juan A. Machado; and in 1866–67 there was an African tango called "El chicova" circulating in Montevideo. Ibid., 152.

4. Bilbao, *Buenos Aires,* 148–149. Pichetti took over the dance studio of Argentine teacher Enrique Foster.

5. Although Donna Guy does not give this number, her breakdown of population, occupations, and origins in Buenos Aires is interesting in relation to the development of the tango. See Guy, *Sex and Danger,* 39–42.

6. Ibid. Guy's book considers many aspects of prostitution in Argentina.

7. Stilman, *Historia del tango,* 32–33. My translation. Here, *Oriental* may refer to a member of a particular military group in Argentina around 1825 whose hats were apparently distinctive enough to be well remembered. This definition appears in some Lunfardo dictionaries.

8. Batiz, *Buenos Aires.* The work is subtitled "Memoirs of a Police Chief." Chavez felt that Batiz wrote the memoir around 1908, possibly in Paris. Chavez's explanatory notes about Batiz's use of slang and his forays through Buenos Aires are included in brackets. The translations are mine.

9. Ibid., 43 ff., 93 ff.

10. See, for example, Castro, *The Argentine Tango,* 30–31.

11. Batiz, *Buenos Aires,* 49 ff.

12. *Mate* is a native tea, traditionally drunk through a filtered straw from a gourd cup. The cup is packed with tea leaves and hot water is added. Often a single cup is passed around at a gathering. It is an acquired taste. As already noted, the *pericone* is a traditional dance of the countryside.

13. The cities referred to are Buenos Aires and Montevideo; the latter is a Uruguayan city that lies across the river from Buenos Aires and contributed many influential composers and performers of the tango.

14. Penon, *The Bandonion.* I detail Penon's thoughts on Paris's influence on Argentine acceptance of the tango in chapter 4.

15. Quoted in Gesualdo, *La musica,* 152. My translation.

16. This series appears on the cover of the sheet music for "El maco," a tango by M. J. Tornquist. Savigliano identifies the man as Arturo de Nava. Savigliano, *Tango,* 154.

17. Castro, *The Argentine Tango,* 17–18. Castro's translation.

18. Drago was the author of the Drago Doctrine, proposed in 1907 at a conference of nations at The Hague. The doctrine states that European countries may not collect debts from countries in the Americas through the use of force. The Porter proposition was adopted instead; it emphasizes arbitration but does not disallow armed intervention.

19. Castro, *The Argentine Tango,* 21–22.

20. Quoted in ibid., 26–28.

21. Quoted in ibid., 38. The quote is from Eusebio Gomez, *La mala vida en Buenos Aires* (Buenos Aires: Argentine Institute of Criminology, 1908), 24–28.

22. Castro, *The Argentine Tango,* 42–43.

23. Eduardo Stilman, *Antologia del verson lunfardo* (Buenos Aires: Editorial Brujula, 1965), 96, quoted in Castro, *The Argentine Tango,* 60.

24. Castro, *The Argentine Tango,* 113.

25. The *zarzuela* is a Spanish operatic form that includes singing, dancing, and spoken dialogue. It first appeared in the mid-seventeenth century.

26. Castro, *The Argentine Tango,* 117.

27. Guy, *Sex and Danger,* 157.

28. Castro, *The Argentine Tango,* 33–34.

29. J. B. Rivera, "Historias paralelas," 39. My translation.

30. The Teatro El Pasatiempo was built in 1887, and at first it offered French operettas, a garden, and a grand salon. After 1890 it was converted into a dance hall for the lower class. Gesualdo, *La Musica,* 153.

31. Savigliano, *Tango,* 37–38. Savigliano believes that the tango could sometimes use sex to level briefly issues of race and class, as in this example from *Justicia criollo,* since Benito and Juanita are of different races.

32. Ibid., 38.

33. Castro, *The Argentine Tango*, 123.

34. Ibid., 127.

35. Gesualdo, *La musica*, 155–156.

36. Sierra, *Historia de la orquesta tipica*, 33.

37. Quoted in Cardenas, "Academias," 27. My translation.

38. Ibid., 26.

39. Ibid.

40. Ibid.

41. Gesualdo, *La musica*, 153. My translation.

42. A photographic reproduction of the single page entitled *Baile de moda* is housed in the Archivo General de la Nación in Buenos Aires. Although one or more of the five photographs appear occasionally in other sources, the original source of the article remains unknown.

43. Cardenas, "Academias," 30.

44. Gesualdo, *La musica*, 152–153.

45. Benaros, "El tango," 268.

46. Cardenas, "Academias," 28. My translation.

47. This is Casimir Ain, who was imported by New York society to teach the tango. His story appears in chapter 2.

48. Castro, *The Argentine Tango*, 101–102.

49. Ibid., 99–100.

2. Europe and the United States Discover the Tango

1. Mouvet, *Art of Dancing*, 85.

2. Curtis Brown, writing for *The Republican* on January 6, 1909, printed on January 17, 1909, no place or newspaper name given. From the clippings file of the dance department of the New York Public Library [hereinafter cited as NYPL].

3. Unidentified article, clippings file, NYPL.

4. Ibid.

5. See Mouvet, *Art of Dancing*, 26–29, for his account of a real *Apache* dance he observed in Paris, and 43–48 for his suggested stage choreography.

6. Ibid., 28–29.

7. Unattributed article, c. 1910, clippings file, NYPL.

8. A humorous historical note is that the *Apache* become a popular stage act in the 1920s, with one adventurous couple even dancing it on ice skates.

9. See appendix 2 for a brief summary of typical headlines of the day.

10. Unattributed article, dated 1914, clippings file, NYPL.

11. Unattributed article, n.d., clippings file, NYPL.

12. Unattributed article, possibly by wire service from Boston, January 17, 1914, clippings file, NYPL.

13. Article from the *Morning Telegraph,* by special dispatch from Boston, January 17, [1914], clippings file, NYPL.

14. Unattributed article, possibly by wire service from Boston, January 23, [1914], clippings file, NYPL.

15. Unattributed and undated article included with others from c. 1914, clippings file, NYPL.

16. Special dispatch to the *Morning Telegraph* from Cleveland on June 12, [1914], clippings file, NYPL.

17. "To the Editor of the New York *Times,*" *New York Times,* January 5, 1914 (Castle), January 8, 1914 (Mack).

18. "To Tango or Not to Tango?" *New York Times,* October 6, 1913, 1.

19. "No Tango at Yale 'Prom,' " *New York Times,* January 23, 1914, 20.

20. Headlines from the *New York Times* index for 1915.

21. "The Cult of the Tango," *Literary Digest,* March 7, 1914, 637–638.

22. "Against the Tango," *Literary Digest,* January 31, 1914, 210.

23. "Tango Shame of Our Days," *New York Times,* January 22, 1914, 4.

24. "Cardinal Cavallari Dead," *New York Times,* November 25, 1914, 11.

25. "Canon Assails Our New Dances," *New York Times,* August 25, 1913, 3.

26. "Tango Teacher Quits Choir," *New York Times,* February 3, 1914, 1.

27. "Dancing Floor Row Splits a Big Church," *New York Times,* June 30, 1914, 20.

28. Castle and Castle, *Modern Dancing,* 155–159.

29. Many of the dance masters who wrote treatises stressed the

core repertoire of six or eight figures that supposedly came from Argentina, and included confirmation of this repertoire by leading performers. See, for example, Clendenen, *Dance Mad,* 9–10; Mouvet, *The Tango,* 7.

30. Crozier, *The Tango,* 77–79.

31. Marguerite Moores Marshall in the *New York Evening World,* November 19, 1913.

32. "Mrs. Fish's Dinner Dance," *New York Times,* June 23, 1914, 11.

33. Marks, *They All Sang,* 155–64. Marks notes that the traditional beverages were fancy cocktails named for favorite performing dancers.

34. Unattributed article, n.d., clippings file, NYPL.

35. Unattributed article, n.d., clippings file, NYPL.

36. "Tango Is Tabooed by Kaiser's Order," *New York Times,* November 18, 1913, 4.

37. "Tango Party Mrs. Astor's," *New York Times,* June 17, 1913, 4.

38. Unattributed article, n.d., clippings file, NYPL.

39. Article with a penciled-in date of November 25, 1913, clippings file, NYPL.

40. Unattributed article, n.d., clippings file, NYPL.

41. Article from the *Manchester Guardian,* possibly 1912 or 1913, clippings file, NYPL.

42. Walker, *Modern Dances,* 11; and Hopkins, *The Tango,* 41.

43. Clendenen, *Dance Mad,* 9.

44. Richardson, *Guide to the Tango,* 5.

45. D'Albert, *Art of Dancing,* 117.

46. Stell y Pellicer, "Tango argentino."

47. Castle and Castle, *Modern Dancing,* 83.

48. Mouvet, *The Tango,* 5; de Fouquières, "Le tango," 10; Koebner, *Tanz brevier,* 34; Pichetti, *La danza antica e moderna,* 149–151.

49. Castle and Castle, *Modern Dancing,* 38.

50. He means *gauchos,* and is apparently confusing *gaucho* with *broncho* (or bronco), an unbroken horse.

51. Mouvet, *The Tango,* 6.

52. Richardson, *Guide to the Tango,* 6–7.

53. Koebner, *Tanz brevier,* 34.

54. Bergen, *Der Tanz,* 36; Clendenen, *Dance Mad,* 9.

55. Pichetti, *La danza antica e moderna,* 149–151.

56. Castle and Castle, *Modern Dancing,* 103.

57. Hopkins, *The Tango,* 66; Mouvet, *Art of Dancing,* 86.

58. Hopkins, *The Tango,* 66.

59. De Fouquières, "Le Tango," 10.

60. Bergen, *Der Tanz,* 36.

61. Walker, *Modern Dances,* 11.

62. Castle and Castle, *Modern Dancing,* 83.

63. Mouvet, *The Tango,* 7.

64. Hopkins, *The Tango,* 66.

3. Argentina Reclaims Its Native Dance

1. Savigliano, *Tango,* 139–140.

2. Castro, *The Argentine Tango,* 93.

3. Benaros, "El tango," 279. My translation.

4. From correspondence with Professor Richard Powers, Stanford University. The translation team was Jade Burns, Maritza Bodine, Elena Melendez, and Luba Petrovich.

5. Castro, *The Argentine Tango,* 177. See also Guy, *Sex and Danger,* for a detailed analysis of the social response to prostitution during this period.

6. Castro, *The Argentine Tango,* 94. Other sources give 1925 as the date of this visit.

7. *Fray Mocho,* May 17, 1912. My translation.

8. Savigliano, *Tango,* 58.

9. Castro, *The Argentine Tango,* 180.

10. Ibid., 83–84.

11. Ibid., 76.

12. See the first epigraph to chapter 4 for a well-known example of Contursi's lyrics.

4. Tango Music

1. Carlos Vega, "El tango andaluz y el tango argentine," *La prensa* (Buenos Aires), April 10, 1932. My translations.

2. Ibid.

3. Ibid.

4. Ibid.

5. Vega does not say what music was contained in the late medieval rabbinical collections. Given the state of notation at that time, it is likely he was using hyperbole to establish the long Hispanic ownership of the habanera.

6. The mazurka disappeared from the common ballroom repertoire by the end of the 1870s, although it continued to appear in dance manuals after 1900. The habanera may have disappeared around the same time or slightly later, as the musical habanera in Buenos Aires came to define the Argentine tango. The polka is one of the longest-lived of the ballroom dances, and Vega's claim that it disappeared is puzzling. People who danced the early tango continued to dance waltzes, *pericones,* and other dances of native Argentina; it is unlikely that they stopped dancing the polka or its late-nineteenth-century version, the two-step.

7. Vega, "El tango andaluz."

8. Matamoro, "Orígenes musicales," 163n. My translation.

9. Stilman, *Historia del tango,* 15–17.

10. Manuel Roman, "Notes on the History of the Bandoneon," quoted in Penon, *The Bandonion,* 39.

11. Ibid.

12. Ibid.

13. Penon, *The Bandonion,* 35.

14. Ibid., 37–38.

15. Gath and Chaves was a large department store in Buenos Aires.

16. According to *Merriam-Webster's Collegiate Dictionary* (11th ed.), to obnubilate oneself means to becloud oneself. Possibly in this context the translator means that the Argentines tried to lose themselves in the ambiance of Paris.

17. It is interesting that these upper-class visitors to Paris embraced the tango partly through homesickness and loneliness—some of the same reasons that lower-class people had embraced it in Argentina.

18. Penon, *The Bandonion,* 57–58.

19. Most tango histories have some biographical information about the more famous composers and performers. See, for example, Stilman,

Historia del tango, 50–93; and de Caro, *El tango in mis recuerdos,* 249–285.

5. Tangos in Waltz Time

1. Markowski, who was a dance master of considerable influence in his own day, is regrettably rather obscure to us, and at this point I can supply neither birth and death dates nor a first name.

2. Durang, *The Fashionable Dancer's Casket,* 151.

3. Yradier, a teacher of composition and solfège at the Madrid Conservatory, spent several years in Paris during the 1850s as a singing teacher to the Empress Eugenie.

4. Both patterns occur with almost equal frequency in the melody of the first sixty-seven bars.

5. Sebastian Yradier, "Maria Dolores" (Paris: Schott, ca. 1870).

6. Marpon, *Markowski and His Ballrooms: Parisian Sketches* (Paris: n.p., 1860). I am indebted to Richard Powers for sharing this source.

7. Curtiss, *Bizet and His World,* 405.

6. The Tango in the World of Art Music

1. Other examples of the tango in art music include Igor Stravinsky's *Histoire du soldat* (1918) and *The Five Fingers* (1920–21), Darius Milhaud's *Saudados do Brasil* (1920–21), Virgil Thompson's *Sonata da chiesa* (1926), Bohuslav Martinu's *Skizzy moderne tancu* (1927), Alban Berg's *Der Wein* (1929), Jean Wiéner's *Cadences pour deux pianos* (1930), and Hans Werner Henze's "Keiner oder Alle" from *Voices* (1973), among many others. The tango also appears in rock and roll and folk music in such works as Weather Report's *American Tango* and Deb Seymour's *Martian Tango.* Even Peter Schickele honored the genre with his *Last Tango in Bayreuth.*

2. See Harding, *Erik Satie,* 126, for more details of this evidence of Satie's views on the connection between money and art.

3. Translated in Gillmor, *Erik Satie,* 177.

4. Milhaud gives the account of staging this production in his memoir, *Notes without Music,* 101–104.

5. Ibid., 117–118. Milhaud's whole account of the various premieres of *Le bœuf* is perhaps more comical than he intended it to be.

6. Howes, *Music of William Walton*, 16. In the original version the first tune is placed to match up simultaneous occurrences of the word *seaside* in both the implied song text and the text of Sitwell's poetry.

7. Stewart, *Ernst Krenek*, 62.

8. Ibid., 83.

9. See ibid., 85, for more analytical details of Křenek's version of jazz in *Jonny spielt auf*.

10. See ibid., 86–89, for critics' remarks and information on various performances.

Bibliography

Adams, Dr. R. A. *The Social Dance.* Kansas City, Kans.: R. A. Adams, 1921.

"The Argentine Tango." *Dance Journal* 5 (July 1913): 3–6.

Bacton, Professor. *Théorie complète et authentique du tango argentin.* [Paris]: n.p., 1912.

Barrionuevo, Leopoldo. *100 anos de tango.* Medellin: Interprint, 1978.

Batiz, Adolfo. *Buenos Aires, la ribera y los prostibulos en 1880.* Ed. A. Chavez. Contribucion a los estudios socials (Libro Rojo). Buenos Aires: Ediciones AGA-Taura, n.d.

Bayo and Chrysis. *Le tango argentin.* [Paris]: n.p., c. 1914.

Benaros, Leon. "El tango y los lugares y cases de baile." *La historia del tango.* Vol. 2. Buenos Aires: Ediciones Corregidor, 1977.

Bergen, Rolfe. *Der Tanz.* Munich: Druck der Innsbrucker Buchdruckerei und Verlagsanstalt, c. 1915.

Bilbao, Manuel. *Buenos Aires, desde su fundacion hasta nuestros dias, especialmente el periodo comprendido en los siglos XVIII y XIX.* Buenos Aires: Juan A. Alsina, 1902.

Cardenas, Daniel J. "Academias, grandes bailarines, caracter de la danza." *Buenos Aires Tango* 3 (January–February 1971).

Carretero, Andres. *El compadrito y el tango.* Buenos Aires: El home de la Argentina commercial, Ediciones Pampa y Cielo, 1964.

Castle, Vernon, and Irene Castle. *Modern Dancing.* New York: Harper and Brothers, 1914.

Castro, Donald. *The Argentine Tango as Social History, 1880-1955.* San Francisco: Edward Mellen Research University Press, 1991.

Charles, D. *Toutes les danses modernes et leurs théories complètes.* Paris: S. Bornemann, 1920s.

Chester, S. Beach. *Secrets of the Tango.* London: T. Werner Laurie, 1914.

Clendenen, F. Leslie. *Dance Mad; Or, the Dances of the Day.* St. Louis: Arcade, 1914.

Cook, Susan C. *Opera for a New Republic: The Zeitopern of Krenek, Weill, and Hindemith.* Ann Arbor: UMI Research Press, 1988.

Crozier, Gladys. *The Tango and How to Dance It.* London: Andrew Melrose, 1913.

Cruz, C. *The Modern Ballroom Tango.* U.S.A.: n.p., 1925.

Curtiss, Mina. *Bizet and His World.* London: Secker & Warburg, 1959.

D'Albert, Charles. *Encyclopedia and Technical Glossary of the Art of Dancing.* London: T. M. Middleton, c. 1914.

Danses nouvelles. Paris: Albin Michel, 1920.

de Caro, Julio. *El tango en mis recuerdos: Su evolucion en la historia.* Buenos Aires: Ediciones Centurion, n.d.

de Fouquières, André. "Le tango." *Dance Journal* 5 (March 1913): 10–11.

de Lara, Tomas. *El tema del tango en la literature Argentina.* Buenos Aires: Ediciones Culturales Argentinas, 1961.

del Priore, Oscar. *El tango de Villoldo a Piazolla.* Buenos Aires: Crisis (Cuadernos de Crisis) no. 13, 1975.

Durang, Charles. *The Fashionable Dancer's Casket.* Philadelphia: Fisher and Brother, 1856.

Faulkner, T. A. *The Lure of the Dance* N.p.: n.p., 1916.

Ferrari, Lidia. *El problema de la autenticidad en el tango. Comentarios sobre "El tango argentine de salón: Método de baile teórico y práctico" de Nicanor Lima, de 1916.* www.buenosairestango.com.

Ferrer, Horacio Arturo. *El libro del tango: Cronica y dictionario, 1850-1977.* Buenos Aires: Editorial Galerna, 1977.

Flitch, J. E. Crawford. *Modern Dancing and Dancers.* London: Grant Richards, 1912.

Garcia—Jiminez, Francisco. *El tango, historia de medio siglo.* Buenos Aires: Editorial Universitaria de Buenos Aires, 1964.

Gesualdo, Vicente. *Historia de la musica en la Argentina.* Vol. 2, *1852-1900.* Buenos Aires: Editorial Beta S.R.L., 1961.

———. *La musica en la Argentina.* Buenos Aires: Editorial Stella, 1988.

Gillmor, Alan M. *Erik Satie.* Boston: Twayne, 1988.

Giovannini, Francesco. *Ballo di ieri e ballo di oggi.* Milan: n.p., 1922.

————. *Ballo d'oggi.* Milan: n.p., 1914.

Giraudet, E. *Méthode moderne de danse.* Paris: n.p., 1914.

Gobello, José. *Diccionario Lunfardo.* Buenos Aires: A. Pena Lillo, Editor S.R.L., 1982.

————. *Las letras del tango de Villoldo a Borges.* [Buenos Aires]: Editorial Brujula, 1966.

————. "Origenes de la letra de tango." *La historia del tango.* Vol. 1. Buenos Aires: Ediciones Corregidor, 1976.

————. "Tango, vocablo controvertido." *La historia del tango.* Vol. 1. Buenos Aires: Ediciones Corregidor, 1976.

Grahame, Robert. "Le tango argentine." *Revue sud-américaine* 1 (1914): 22–30.

Guy, Donna. *Sex and Danger in Buenos Aires: Prostitution, Family, and Nation in Argentina.* Lincoln: University of Nebraska Press, 1991.

Harding, James. *Erik Satie.* New York: Praeger, 1975.

Hopkins, J. S. *The Tango and Other Up-to-Date Dances.* Chicago: Saalfield, 1914.

Howe, Elias. *The American Dancing Master.* Boston: Russell and Tolman, 1862.

Howes, Frank. *The Music of William Walton.* London: Oxford University Press, 1965.

Humphrey, Walter. "How to Dance the Tango." *Ballroom Dancing Times* (London, 1911); reprinted in *Ballroom Dancing Times,* October 1990, 12–13.

Jakubs, Deborah. "From Bawdyhouse to Cabaret: The Evolution of Tango as an Expression of Argentine Popular Culture." *Journal of Popular Culture* 18 (1984): 133–145.

Kinney, Troy, and Margaret Kinney. *The Dance: Its Place in Art and Life.* New York: n.p., 1914.

————. *Social Dancing of To-Day.* New York: n.p., 1914.

Koebner, F. W. *Das Tanz-Brevier.* Berlin: Verlag Dr. Eysler, 1913.

LeFort, Charles. *L'art de la danse.* Paris: n.p., 1911.

Lipesker, Felix, ed. *Julio de Caro: 10 variaciones para bandoneon de sus obras mas populares.* Album no. 4, Biblioteca del Bandoneonista. Industria Argentina, Casa Liscio, n.d.

Marks, Edward. *They All Sang: From Tony Pastor to Rudy Vallee*. New York: Viking, 1934.

Matamoro, Blas. "Origenes musicales." *La historia del tango*. Vol. 1. Buenos Aires: Ediciones Corregidor, 1976.

Milhaud, Darius. *Notes without Music: The Autobiography of Darius Milhaud*. New York: Knopf, 1953.

Miller, Stanley. *The Tango as Danced in the Ballroom*. n.p.: George Anderson, 1914.

Minchin, Madame. *Théorie du tango argentin*. Paris: Durand, 1912.

Mouvet, Maurice. *Maurice's Art of Dancing*. New York: Schirmer, 1915.

—————. *The Tango and the New Dances*. Chicago: Laird and Lee, 1914.

Newman, Albert. *Dances of Today*. Philadelphia: Penn, 1914.

Orquesta Tipica "Victor." Ed. Nestor Sabato. Buenos Aires: Coleccion los grandes del tango, ano 1, numero 41, 1991.

Penon, Arturo, with Mendez, Javier Garcia. *The Bandonion: A Tango History. A Memoir of Arturo Penon*. Trans. Tim Barnard. London, Ont.: Nightwood Editions, 1988.

Peters, A. *Le tango: Les nouveaux pas du tango*. Paris: Editions Nilsson, c. 1920s.

Pichetti, E. *La danza antica e moderna*. Rome: n.p., 1914.

Les 15 danses modernes. France/Algiers: n.p., c. 1920s.

Raymond, Paul. "The Argentine Tango." *Dance Journal* 4 (January 1912): 11–12.

Richardson, P. J. S., ed. *The Guide to the Tango*. London: Francis, Day and Hunter, c. 1914.

Rivera, Jorge B. "Historias paralelas." *La historia del tango*. Vol. 1. Buenos Aires: Ediciones Corregidor, 1976.

Rivera, Max. *Le tango et les danses nouvelles*. Paris: Pierre LaFitte, 1913.

Robert, L. *Théorie du vrai tango argentin*. Paris: Salabert, c. 1911.

Robert, M. "The Tango." *Dance Journal* 5 (March 1913): 4.

Sabato, Ernesto. *Tango: Canción de Buenos Aires*. Buenos Aires: Editiones Centro Arte, 1964.

Savigliano, Marta E. *Tango and the Political Economy of Passion*. Boulder: Westview Press, 1995.

Scobie, James. *Argentina: A City and a Nation*. New York: Oxford University Press, 1964.

Selles, Roberto. "El tango y sus dos primeras decadas, 1880–1900." *La historia del tango.* Vol. 2. Buenos Aires: Ediciones Corregidor, 1977.

Sheafe, Alfonso. *The Fascinating Boston.* Boston: Boston Music Company, 1913.

Sierra, Luis Adolfo. *Historia de la orquesta tipica: Evolution instrumental del tango.* Ed. A. Pena Lillo. Coleccion La Siringa, no. 36. Buenos Aires: n.p., 1966.

Steinke, A., with Willi Weissbart. *Tango Galiziano.* Berlin: Orpheus Verlag, c. 1914.

Stell y Pellicer. "Tango argentino." In *Danzas modernas.* Madrid: Antonio Izquierdo, 1915.

Stewart, John L. *Ernst Krenek: The Man and His Music.* Berkeley: University of California Press, 1991.

Stilman, Eduardo. *Historia del tango.* Buenos Aires: Editorial Brujula, 1965.

Swepstone, Eileen. *The Tango.* Vancouver, B.C.: J. H. Welch, 1914.

Taylor, Julie. "Tango: Theme of Class and Nation." *Journal of Ethnomusicology* 20 (1976): 273–291.

"The Truth about the Tango." *Dancing Times,* August 1913, 691–694.

Vade mecum du parfait danseur: Les danses en vogue. Paris: F. D. Marchetti, 1920.

Vidart, Daniel. *El tango y su mundo.* Montevideo: Ediciones Tauro, 1964.

Von Bruch, Henry W. *The Carnival of Death.* New York: The Book Stall, 1920.

Walker, Caroline. *The Modern Dances: How to Dance Them.* Chicago: Saul Brothers, 1914.

Walton, Susana. *William Walton: Behind the Façade.* New York: Oxford University Press, 1988.

Zucchi, Oscar. "El bandoneon en el tango." *La historia del tango.* Vol. 5. Buenos Aires: Ediciones Corregidor, 1977.

Index

Italicized page numbers indicate illustrations.

Jo Baim lives in Seattle, where she is Assistant Organist at historic Trinity Parish Episcopal Church and a freelance choreographer. She is an Oblate of the Benedictine Monastery of St. Gertrude in Cottonwood, Idaho. For ten years she was the founder and artistic director of The Seaside Pavilion Historic Dance Society in Seattle, where she taught historic ballroom dance as a social pastime and choreographed for a costumed performing troupe. Jo is owned by Henry Cecil, a phenomenal German shepherd, who is a nursing home therapy dog and a brave survivor of canine lymphoma.